The Hyperactive Child Book

Also by Leif Terdal, Ph.D. (with Eric J. Mash, Ph.D.)

Behavioral Assessment of Childhood Disorders

The Hyperactive Child Book

A Pediatrician, a Child Psychologist, and a Mother Team Up to Offer the Most Practical, Up-to-Date Guide to Treating, Educating, and Living with Your ADHD Child

By
Patricia Kennedy,
Leif Terdal, Ph.D.,
and
Lydia Fusetti, M.D.

St. Martin's Press
New York

THE HYPERACTIVE CHILD BOOK. Copyright © 1993 by Patricia Kennedy, Leif Terdal, Ph.D., and Lydia Fusetti, M.D. All rights reserved. Printed in the United States of America. No part of this book may be used or reproduced in any manner whatsoever without written permission except in the case of brief quotations embodied in critical articles or reviews. For information, address St. Martin's Press, 175 Fifth Avenue, New York, N.Y. 10010.

Library of Congress Cataloging-in-Publication Data

Kennedy, Patricia.
The hyperactive child book / Patricia Kennedy, Leif Terdal, and Lydia Fusetti.
    p.   cm.
Includes bibliographical references and index.
ISBN 0-312-11286-6 (pbk.)
1. Attention-deficit hyperactivity disorder—Popular works. 2. Hyperactive children. I. Terdal, Leif, G., 1937- . II. Fusetti, Lydia. III. Title.
RJ506.H9K45   1994
649'.153—dc20
                                                                    94-18493
                                                                    CIP

Excerpt from *Peterson's Guides to Colleges for Learning-Disabled Students*, 2nd edition, edited by Charles T. Mangrum and Stephen S. Strichart. Copyright © 1988 by Peterson's Guides. Reprinted by permission of the publisher.

First Paperback Edition: September 1994
10 9 8 7 6 5 4 3 2 1

We would like to dedicate this book to the parents, the children, and the educators and other professionals who are open enough to try new methods of helping ADHD children live happier, fuller lives.

About the Authors

PATRICIA KENNEDY has done graduate work in education and psychology and is the mother of two children. After her son Max was diagnosed as having ADHD and learning disabilities, she sought assistance from her coauthors, psychologist Dr. Leif Terdal and pediatrician Dr. Lydia Fusetti. With the help of his family, his doctors, and the techniques described in this book, Max became an honors student in high school, garnered top SAT scores, and is now studying computer science in college.

LEIF TERDAL, Ph.D., is a professor of medical psychology at Oregon Health Sciences University and has coauthored and contributed to several books, including *Behavioral Assessment of Childhood Disorders* and *Handbook of Clinical Behavioral Pediatrics.*

LYDIA FUSETTI, M.D., practices general pediatrics and is a courtesy professor at Oregon State University's Department of Motor Disabilities, as well as a consulting specialist in child development for the state of Oregon.

The authors live near Portland, Oregon.

Acknowledgments

We would like to thank our agent, Natasha Kern, and our editors, Hope Dellon and Jenny Notz. Their professional talent and encouragement brought this book to fruition.

A number of people have contributed in major ways to the preparation of this book. Dr. John Keiter provided invaluable technical assistance in preparing this manuscript for publication. We thank Dr. Melvin Levine, who teaches doctors to look at the child as a total person, for sharing his knowledge; and Drs. Russell Barkley and Eric Mash, for their help. We wish to thank Drs. Marjorie Terdal, Ingrid Leckliter, Gloria Krahn, Ann Garner, Darryn Sikora, Jeff Sosne, James Lindemann, and Russell Jackson for editorial feedback on the manuscript and Drs. Sarojini Budden and LeRoy Carlson for teaching residents and others who work with ADHD children. We thank the entire LD team at C.D.R.C. in Portland: John Hale, Darryl Anderson, Donald Nelson, Sue Wright, Jerry Smith, Pat Haley, Chris Williams, and LeRoy Carlson, in addition to other members we already mentioned. We thank the staff of the Corvallis Children's Clinic for their patience, and we thank our readers: Linda Varsell-Smith, Patricia Melugin-Cousins, Susan R. Nelson, Nancy Matsumoto, Elizabeth Oliver, Iona Lockwood, Peggy Hansen, Cindy Klein, Jaap Leegwater, Jolie Mayer-Smith, Ph.D., Linda Teslik, LeRoy Carlson, M.D., Christopher P.S. Williams, M.D., Robert Nickel, M.D., and Eldon Younger, M.D. Finally, we would like to thank our families: Tim, Max, and Marie Kennedy, Marge, Erik, and Paul Terdal, and Rosie, Al, and Carl Fusetti.

Contents

Introduction

As a mother waits in her pediatrician's office she tries to read to her squirming five-year-old son, Adam. With kicking feet and a wiggling body, Adam breaks free from his mother's restraining embrace and heads for the fish tank, knocking over the philodendron on his way. Mom scrambles to straighten the plant and clean up the dirt. While she's doing that, Adam swishes his hands in the tank's water. "Adam, get out of there." But Adam doesn't stop until Mom pulls his hands from the water. She dries his hands on the Kleenex from her purse, and before she can stuff the tissue back into her purse or even get back to the plant dirt on the floor, Adam sweeps every magazine from the doctor's display rack onto the floor. While his slow speech development worries her, Adam's mother is most concerned about her son's behavior. The doctor takes one look at Adam, his tired mother, and his waiting room and decides that Adam is hyperactive. His diagnosis will be reinforced by what Adam's mother tells him: "His kindergarten teacher says he's hyperactive and that Ritalin might help." While his pediatrician may be an excellent doctor, he doesn't have the equipment necessary to do extensive hearing evaluations in his office. Adam is about to be placed on Ritalin for a hearing problem that would respond better to using a hearing aid along with speech therapy than to medication.

Specialists who work with hyperactive children (developmental pediatricians, pediatric neurologists, child psychiatrists, and child psychologists) are quick to tell you that attention problems, including Attention Deficit–Hyperactivity Disorder (ADHD), are not as simple to diagnosis as we once thought. As a parent you need to know that there are many kinds of attention problems, some of them leading to hyperactive behavior, which are not true ADHD. Patricia Kennedy, one of the coauthors of this book, spent seven years between her son Max's first diagnosis of ADHD and the final diagnosis of ADHD with learning disabilities and motor dyspraxia. (Motor dyspraxia is a term that describes a neurological problem that interferes with motor output. A motor dyspraxia problem with regard to writing would affect both speed and legibility of the penmanship.) During that time the family and the child wasted valuable time and a great deal of money trying to figure out what was wrong and what steps should be taken to work on the problems.

All parents of hyperactive children worry: Will my child be all right? How can I do what is best for my child? Parents feel guilty if they have their child on medication and guilty if they do not. Most parents hunger for information, answers, and most of all, understanding of their child and the disorder.

This book is an effort to help you understand ADHD and other attention problems and to provide you with information about helping your hyperactive child. It is our hope that in helping your child to do better, you will also be helping yourself. In the following pages we present the latest research and the practical day-to-day information you will need to raise your hyperactive child.

In 1982 the authors of this book were involved in the team assessment of Max. While other professionals were involved in the assessment phase as well, Pat Kennedy, developmental pediatrician Dr. Lydia Fusetti, and child psychologist Dr. Leif Terdal have remained an ongoing management team. Together with school personnel they have helped Max through school and into college. During his high-school years, Max was on the honor roll, and won math awards, as well as a scholarship. He is currently a university junior majoring in computer science.

ADHD: What It Is and How It Is Treated

Exactly What Is Attention Deficit—Hyperactivity Disorder?

In this book we use the term hyperactivity as shorthand for Attention Deficit–Hyperactivity Disorder (ADHD). Although we intend the information to apply to girls as well as boys, we also use the pronoun "he."

There are three main characteristics of ADHD: impulsivity, inability to pay attention, and hyperactivity. One of these three characteristics—inability to pay attention—is also found in a related disorder called Attention Deficit Disorder (ADD). It is important for parents to realize that a child can have this disorder and not be hyperactive. Children who are both impulsive and inattentive have more problems than ADD children. Whereas ADD and ADHD are not the same disorder, they are part of a spectrum of attention problems ranging from mild ADD to severe ADHD. They respond to the same medications and behavioral management programs. For that reason, the behavioral management programs, techniques, and ideas presented in this book work equally well with ADD children.

What Are the Three Main Characteristics of ADHD?

Impulsivity

This is most often seen when the child does things without thinking first: running out in the street, hitting another child, taking apart a toy, or blurting out an answer in class without being called on. These children have difficulty waiting their turn and following rules.

Inability to Pay Attention

ADHD and ADD children seem to have difficulty paying attention both at school and at home. Teachers and parents report that the child can be told something "a million times," and the child still does not seem to understand. Children who are unable to pay attention become frustrated easily and give up if they are not successful right away.

Hyperactivity

Hyperactivity means "overactivity." Hyperactive children are wound up tighter than a twenty-four hour clock starting its first minute. Parents frequently describe their hyperactive children "as if they were driven by a motor."

Hyperactivity is very different from having a high energy level. People with a focused high energy level can accomplish enormous amounts of work. Hyperactive people are very busy, but they do not accomplish much.

Diagnosing ADHD

Professionals use a process that looks at a number of different causes and problems from as many angles as possible. They rule out one set of possibilities at a time until they reach a diagnosis. This process of examination and elimination is called differential diagnosis. The professionals who work with hyperactive children look for the following criteria to sort out children with Primary ADHD from children with other attention problems.

- At least two sources (parents, teachers, or doctors) reported that the child has poor attention span, poor impulse control, poor compliance with instructions, poor self-control, and poor rule-governed behavior. (Poor rule-governed behavior means that the child knows what will happen if he breaks the rules but cannot control himself and breaks them anyway.)
- The behavior problems have placed the child in the top 3 percent for symptoms of ADHD as compared with other children of the same age and sex.
- The child has exhibited symptoms for at least six months to a year.
- The behavioral symptoms began in early childhood and before five years of age. (Teenagers, for instance, who suddenly develop symptoms of ADHD may have hormonal or environmental changes that cause attention problems, not Primary ADHD.)
- The symptoms are ongoing and occur in multiple settings. (For example, they don't just occur in reading class but in math and other classes as well.)
- The child has an IQ of 70 or higher; if mentally retarded, the child must be compared with other children of similar mental age for behavioral assessment.
- The diagnosis of Primary ADHD excludes the following causes:

mental retardation

deafness

blindness

gross brain damage

severe language delay

childhood psychosis

autism

cerebral palsy

severe emotional disturbances

Over the past few decades the disorder has been called by many names, including hyperactivity, minimal brain dysfunctions (MBD), hyperkinesis, and Attention Deficit Disorder (ADD). Attention Deficit–Hyperactivity Disorder represents the currently accepted term, though the name is bound to change yet again.

Usually a child with ADHD has many of the following symptoms, which are common to people with attention problems. However, many individuals (with attention problems but without ADHD) have some of the problems on this list.[1]

- *Purposeless selection of stimuli*—listens to the air conditioner instead of the math lesson
- *Weak resistance to distraction*—easily distracted by all types of stimuli
- *Impersistence*—is unable to stick with a task (gives up very easily)
- *Inefficiences of motor activity*—or unproductive overactivity: on the go, but going nowhere
- *Insatiability*—wants all the toys in the toy box, but when he has them, demands more
- *Impulsivity*—acts without thinking
- *Academic failure*—poor school work
- *Social failure*—poor peer relations, difficulty making or keeping friends
- *Performance inconsistency*—has good days and bad days. Some days he understands his math with no problems; the next day, the same material is like a foreign language
- *Attention difficulties*—has trouble staying on task
- *Diminished self-esteem*—feels badly about himself
- *Disorganization*—difficulty in organizing how to do tasks

Scanning the list of symptoms, you can see why a checklist alone is not enough to diagnose Primary ADHD. Sally and Bennett Shaywitz, both pediatricians at Yale's School of Medicine, have estimated that 10 to 20 percent of the school-age population has some type of attention problem.[2] While some estimates of attention problems in the general population run as high as 25 percent, most researchers agree that only 3 to 5 percent of the general population are ADHD.

Identifying the ADHD Child

It is important for parents, physicians, and mental health workers to distinguish between other kinds of attention problems and true ADHD. Correct diagnosis is crucial for decisions affecting long-term management or treatment and whether or not medication should be used. Therefore, throughout this book, you will find we stress the multidisciplinary team assessment of attention problems.

Team assessments are done at a number of places, and we have listed some of them in Appendix C of this book. Many universities with medical schools have child development centers connected to them that conduct learning disorders clinics. At a learning disorders clinic, professionals from a number of fields look at children who are having difficulty learning at school or at home. The examination consists of different tests designed to uncover the underlying problem or weakness. After each professional conducts tests in his particular specialty, the members of the team meet and pool their results and insights.

Attention Problems

There are various kinds of attention problems that stem from other causes. Although many attention problems bring about ADHD-like symptoms, only Primary ADHD is intrinsic (the child is born that way).

Primary Attention Deficit–Hyperactivity Disorder

How is Primary ADHD Different from the Other Attention Problems?

The three major criteria for diagnosis of Primary ADHD are behavioral difficulties shown by decreased attention, increased impulsivity, and hyperactivity when compared to children of the same age, sex, and intelligence level.[3]

John:
Primary ADHD

John's mother came into her pediatrician's office requesting a cage for her son. John, seven years old and her third child, was in constant motion, impulsive, and unable to follow any directions. If he was asked to go to his room to pick up his blue shirt and place it in the hamper, he would be found playing in his room with the shirt still on the floor. He was on the move even before he was born, being her most active child in utero. John never seemed to have a schedule, seldom needed sleep, and could be found wandering the house during the night after he mastered climbing out of his crib. Discipline did not seem to work, nor did all the parenting techniques used on the other two boys. He never stayed on the time-out chair, and spankings did no good. John seemed totally oblivious to his behavior: he would be eating a piece of forbidden cake and with the cake in his hand, would deny any knowledge of having taken it. He never finished anything he started and, except for sitting down long enough to play a video game, never watched TV except on the run.

His major problems in school were staying on task and keeping track of what was happening in the classroom. While he was capable of doing the assignment, he would forget to take home the book he needed for his homework. When he completed his homework, he would forget to put the homework in his backpack or forget to hand it in when he was in class.

He could be incredibly observant and recall details long after the event—months later he could recall what color tie Uncle Joe wore on Christmas—but could seldom remember the page of his spelling assignment. His mother requested a cage after he handed his two-year-old brother a book of matches to play with and showed him how to strike them. Both parents complained that if John had been born first, he would have been an only child. John is a child with Primary ADHD. Primary ADHD children are very distractible and have trouble filtering out everyday sounds like the air conditioner or the voices of other children on the playground. They have difficulty self-monitoring their work habits and their social behavior. Vigilance, or maintaining a level of performance over a period of time, is a problem as well. Sometimes they do not spend enough time on a task (impersistence) and other times they become so involved in a task they are unwilling to leave it.

Moreover, the ADHD child may have associated problems such as bed-wetting, fecal soiling, or sleep disorders. From 30 to 60 percent of ADHD children have poor or immature coordination.[4] Doctors also report that some ADHD children have more ear infections, colds, and allergies. Experts like Dr. Russell Barkley and Dr. Melvin Levine have reviewed studies on ear infections in ADHD children. Although the reasons remain unclear, the research seems to indicate a connection between repeated episodes of ear infections and neurodevelopmental disorders like ADHD.[5] Also, ADHD children may have problems making and keeping friends, perhaps because they do not pick up on social cues given by other children or because they are so impulsive that they are constantly in trouble with their playmates.

What Kinds of Other Problems Cause Attention Problems?

Dr. Melvin Levine,[6] a developmental pediatrician and researcher, breaks down attention problems into five groups:

Primary attention deficit
Secondary attention deficit
Situational inattention
Intended inattention
Mixed forms

We have already seen a primary attention deficit–hyperactive child in John, but there are four other kinds of attention problems. The remaining attention problems are brought on by something extrinsic to the child.

SECONDARY ATTENTION DEFICIT

Some children, like Adam in our Introduction, have problems that cause inattention and make them appear hyperactive. They have a problem that causes secondary inattention and hyperactive behavior. Let us look at a second case: David's case.

David: ADHD or Hearing Problems? David was referred to the learning disorders clinic for a multidisciplinary evaluation. He was not functioning well in school, and the teachers and the principal thought he might be hyperactive. He was disruptive in class and pestered other children during quiet time. During class assignments he tried to peek at other students' papers. He finished his papers incorrectly, despite his teacher's multiple attempts to talk with him and give additional help. Although David did poorly in school, he still liked school, and he was exceptionally talented in art class and at building projects. When performing these tasks, he was in "a world of his own" and would spend more than the required time on favorite assignments. In addition to believing he was hyperactive, his teachers felt he was a very visual child. The latter observation proved correct. The major finding in the team assessment at the clinic was that David had a moderate hearing loss that made verbal learning difficult for him. His attempts to see his classmate's papers were not done as impulsive or attention-seeking behavior but rather to find out what he was supposed to be doing, since he could not hear the directions.

A **Secondary Attention Deficit** is seen when a child has another problem that causes difficulty paying attention. In David's case it was a hearing problem. When David could not hear, he grabbed papers, acted up, and behaved in some ways that made his teachers and parents think he might be hyperactive. Usually secondary attention problems can be "cured" by treating the underlying cause. In David's case a hearing aid took care of his problem and ended the inattention.

Emotional problems can also cause attention problems, creating another kind of secondary attention deficit. Lori is an example.

Lori: ADHD or Emotional Problems?

Seven-year-old Lori started having trouble in second grade. She had been in the top reading group in first grade, but second-grade reading was a struggle. Lori was easily distracted and her work became careless and incomplete. She had two or three good friends in first grade, but this year she had none, since she would hit the other children at the least provocation. Her second-grade teacher was beginning to think Lori might be hyperactive.

Further investigation revealed that Lori's parents were going through a messy divorce. Lori's attention problems were brought on by the emotional and social problems she was dealing with at home with her mom and dad. The diagnostic team looked at Lori and found two tip-offs. Lori had no symptoms of hyperactivity before age seven, and a change occurred in her social adjustment as well as her academic skills. Helping Lori deal with her family problems eliminated her behavior problems and inattention.

SITUATIONAL INATTENTION

Situational inattention is seen when circumstances extrinsic to the child, such as inappropriate expectations, perceptions, or educational circumstances, cause the child to have difficulty paying attention. The child is asked to attend to a task that is far beyond his capability, a situation rather like asking an average adult to pay attention in an advanced physics class or a rocket design class. The situation is what brings on symptoms of ADHD. With this type of inattention, the problem of paying attention occurs **only** in specific situations or settings. Such was the case with Martha.

Martha: ADHD or Situational Inattention?

Martha, age two and a half, "does not obey and grabs things," according to her parents.

Mr. and Mrs. Robinson brought Martha to a psychologist for a consultation. They reported that often Martha did not obey. She threw terrible temper tantrums and had "a mind of her own." The father added, "My wife and I can't even read to her. She just grabs things."

The psychologist wanted to observe Martha in a situation that was as natural as possible for her. He brought the parents and Martha to a playroom in the clinic. In one wall of the room was a one-way mirror through which the psychologist could observe. The parents were asked to think of the session as a time when they could play with their child without being interrupted by phone calls or other distractions.

Some time into the session, Mr. Robinson picked up a picture book and suggested, "Martha, let me read to you." Martha came over and sat next to her father. As he opened the book, she reached for the page. "No! Keep your hands off the book. Sit and listen while I read!" Martha reached again, trying to touch the objects on the page. "No, get your hands off," Mr. Robinson repeated in a louder voice. He never did read the book. Instead he repeated, "Don't! Stop that!" Martha slapped at the book and walked away.

A little while later, the psychologist interviewed the parents about their child's behavior and their own behavior toward her. The father commented on Martha's unruly behavior when he tried to read to her. The psychologist noted that most children her age would act in a similar way. They may show interest by "touching" various objects on a page, and they may not be ready to hear anything about a story until they have "looked" the page over with both eyes and fingers. The psychologist encouraged Mr. Robinson to reenter the room with his daughter and try again to "read" to Martha, this time allowing her to touch the page and even commenting as she showed interest.

The father reentered the room and reintroduced a book. Martha came over, reached for a page, and pointed with glee to a picture of a duck. This time instead of correcting his daughter, Mr. Robinson said, "Yes, you see a duck! I wonder who he is and what he's doing?" After a pause, he let her turn the page. After "looking" at the pages with eyes and fingers she was ready to listen as her father talked about the stories in the pictures.

Martha's "problem" of inattention and impulsivity was normal for her age. There was a mismatch of her father's expectations and her age (mismatch of expectation over ability). She was not ADHD. Rather, she needed her parents to be responsive to her at *her* developmental level. Her father also showed that he could change his behavior toward his child. After her father's behavior changed, Martha became more cooperative.

INTENDED INATTENTION

This type of attention problem is a conscious strategy adopted by a child to avoid humiliation when the child is faced with a specific task in which he is weak. Children are survivors: they learn to do what is necessary to avoid embarrassment and to protect their self-esteem. Children sometimes use inattention as a conscious strategy to avoid humiliation in areas of weakness or to avoid tasks in areas beyond their abilities. Let's look at Robert's case.

Robert: ADHD or Intended Inattention

When Robert was called upon to read in his social studies class, he was embarrassed, because he went to the resource room for special help in reading and was almost two years behind in his reading ability. Unfortunately, the substitute teacher has not been told this, so Robert feigned inattention, became the class clown, and declared loudly that he did not need to learn about social studies. He achieved the desired result: He was disciplined but not humiliated by his inability to read.

Intended inattention is seen only in specific settings or situations. Robert was never a problem in gym class, shop, or music, where reading was not required. His problems arose in areas where he had an underlying weakness. He used his "inattention" as a conscious strategy or learned behavior to avoid humiliation.

MIXED FORM OF INATTENTION

When children have attention problems caused by two or more of the types, they are said to have a **mixed form of inattention.** Such a child may have a primary attention deficit and an additional problem such as a learning disability, a visual problem, or an emotional problem. The case of Max is a good example of a mixed form of inattention.

Max: Mixed Form of Inattention

Pat Kennedy's son Max was four years old when his local pediatrician diagnosed him as hyperactive. Though Max could add single-digit numbers at four, his speech development was unusual and behind that of other children his age. He had trouble with pen-and-paper tasks. At age five and a half, Max had surgery to correct problems from repeated ear infections. With improved hearing, his ability to speak improved, too.

When he started school, he ran into more difficulties. School personnel repeatedly told Pat that Max was retarded. Because of Max's skill in some areas, she did not believe them. A series of tests given by the school proved Pat was correct. However, the school still was not sure what was wrong with Max. The school strongly suspected he might be emotionally disturbed. His mother and pediatrician both disagreed with that.

After Dr. Fusetti, a developmental pediatrician, moved to town, she evaluated Max and made a referral to a diagnostic team for further evaluation. From the team's evaluation, a true picture of Max emerged. Max had Primary ADHD, learning disabilities, and motor dyspraxia. For Max it had been seven very hard years between his first diagnosis and his last. For his parents, it was seven years of wasted time and money and missed opportunities: time when they could have been doing something to help but did not know what to do. Perhaps if the multidisiciplinary team evaluation had been done at five or six years of age, those seven years of dismay and feeling of frustration would have been eliminated.

In all of the cases we have examined, the children were originally thought to be ADHD by parents, teachers, physicians, or psychologists. None of them had Primary ADHD, except Max who had a mixed form. All of them could have been placed on medication, and the medication would not have solved the underlying source of their attention problems.

OTHER FACTORS TO RULE OUT

In arriving at an accurate diagnosis of ADHD, professionals must evaluate for physical problems such as hearing loss, poor eyesight, and for mental retardation, as well as learning disabilities. Learning disabilities include the following:

> *Visual-perceptual problems*   understanding information the child sees
>
> *Language disabilities*   difficulties with written or spoken language
>
> *Deficits in sequential organization*   keeping things in the correct order
>
> *Short-term memory problems*   inability to remember chunks of information for short periods of time; a child with a memory problem may only be able to remember a one-part command, whereas most children of the same age could do a three- or four-part command without difficulty
>
> *Signs of neuromaturational delay*   includes delays in ability to tell right from left compared to other children, or motor incoordination.[7]

Learning-disabled children may have one of these weaknesses, or they may have a number of them. The weaknesses may cause attention problems—secondary attention deficit—in school and may contribute to poor self-esteem or conduct problems. A child with just these problems would be considered a learning-disabled child and not an ADHD child, yet some primary ADHD children do have learning disabilities in addition to the ADHD. Learning-disabled children need special help in school as their primary therapy.

Temperament

Another influence on a child's behavior is his temperament. Just as children are born with blue eyes or brown hair, they are born with a temperament that is intrinsic. Stella Chess and Alexander Thomas did a twelve-year study on the temperamental development of children[8] that examined their different temperamental types: the easy child, the slow to warm-up child, and the difficult child. Difficult children are hard for parents and teachers to handle. Placed in a classroom situation with a "poor fit," a difficult child could be mistaken for a hyperactive child by an incompatible teacher, and the same holds true for the home with incompatible parents. Laid-back parents may find it difficult to parent an intense, high-energy child. Because of the role temperament plays in the child's behavior, both the child's temperament and those of his caretakers should be considered.

When Should a Parent Take a Child in for an Evaluation?

Most parents are like John's mother. They put up with the "difficult" behavior of the child until a somewhat serious incident occurs at home (such as the child giving his brother matches) or until the school requests a medical diagnosis. About 50 percent of people who have received a diagnosis of ADHD showed enough disruptive and out-of-control behavior by age four to prompt their parents to seek help for the child from a physician or mental health worker. Sometimes it is the kindergarten teacher who notices the inattention and the overactive behavior and encourages parents to seek professional help. Beginning school also brings a large group of children together, and parents begin to look at their child's behavior in comparison to that of other children of the same age and sex. In general, parents should take the child in for evaluation if they feel the child has problems with impulsivity, inattention, and hyperactivity **and** if someone else, like the teacher or the physician, also feels the child is having trouble with the same three things in comparison to other children of the same age, sex, and mental ability.

Sometimes parents and teachers both feel there is a possibility the child may be ADHD but delay referral because "Bobby is not as bad as Johnny, who already has been diagnosed as ADHD." It is always best to seek professional help as soon as you have the slightest suspicion your child has attention problems.

Degrees of ADHD

ADHD may occur in a greater or lesser degree of severity, making a difference in the child's behavior. Children vary in the severity of the symptoms and in how much difficulty the ADHD causes them in their everyday life. We use the words *mild, moderate,* and *severe* to describe the severity of hyperactivity.

MILD

Children with mild ADHD show behavioral symptoms that meet the criteria for a diagnosis of ADHD but show only mild problems in school and in their relationships with others.

MODERATE

People with moderate ADHD have significant problems at home, at school, and with peers. They require ongoing intervention and reevaluations from time to time. Coexisting problems such as learning disabilities or oppositional defiant behavior may be present. (*Oppositional defiant behavior* refers to a pattern of very negative and argumentative behavior.) Children who show very high rates of acting up and disruptive behavior usually also show low self-esteem and low frustration tolerance.

SEVERE

Children with severe cases of ADHD have significant and widespread problems functioning at home, at school, and in getting along with others. The coexisting problems of conduct disorder and/or learning disabilities are almost always present in these cases.

Naturally, children in the mild range do better than those in the severe category. Children with only mild ADHD may not need medication and may respond to behavioral management alone. Children with mild ADHD may function well as adults without major impairment. With maturity and learned skills, many ADHD children can overcome their disability and lead normal, productive lives.

Will My Child Outgrow ADHD?

Not so long ago we thought that about 60 percent of all ADHD children would outgrow the disorder. What we were observing was the visible decline in the overactivity (the hyperactive motor component) part of the disorder. This made parents and researchers alike think that children outgrew ADHD. New technologies and long-term research now indicate that this is not the case. Professionals now think that only 30 to 40 percent of children with ADHD outgrow it as adults, and they are usually the mild cases. Overactivity may decline, but problems with inattention and impulsivity remain. As children with mild ADHD mature and gain more social and intellectual control, they may experience only slightly more difficulty than their "normal" friends. For many children, ADHD will remain a lifelong problem requiring extra techniques for coping successfully with life. Fortunately, we now know many techniques that work at school and at home. One of the goals of this book is to share those techniques with parents.

What Causes ADHD, or "Is It My Fault?"

Learning that your child has a disability can be a frightening experience. You are filled with concerns for your child and for yourself. After learning that their child has ADHD, most parents' first question is, "What causes ADHD?"

Mr. and Mrs. Jones obtained an appointment for their seven-year-old son at a pediatric clinic at Oregon Health Sciences University. The parents explained to the medical resident that they had been concerned about their son's behavior since he was three years old; their concerns had worsened with recent reports of poor school performance. Their son cooperated during a vision and hearing screening and a pediatric evaluation. Additionally, the medical resident reviewed a recent psychological evaluation and behavioral rating from the school. He interviewed Mr. and Mrs. Jones about family history and the child's early development and behavioral patterns.

The medical resident and supervising pediatrician reviewed the findings with the parents and gave the diagnosis as ADHD. This diagnosis was not a surprise to the parents, and they approved a plan to manage difficult day-to-day situations.

The parents then asked the question about cause: "What has caused our son to be so active and impulsive, and have such a short attention span?" The physician responded, "There is no known cause in this case."

Nevertheless, though the issue of cause is often a moot one for parents whose child has been diagnosed as ADHD, it occasionally helps to examine known causes. Knowledge of known causes enables parents to have something to go on in assessing the work of the diagnosticians, especially in instances in which a diagnosis seems questionable.

ADHD is a Disorder Defined by Clinical Symptoms and Not by Cause

There is no single cause of ADHD. There are a large number of biological or neurological events that singly or in combination can cause a person to be unable to pay attention and be overactive and exhibit other symptoms of ADHD. Because a large number of things can cause ADHD, the disorder is defined by clinical symptoms—or a cluster of behaviors of attention deficit, impulsivity, overactivity. ADHD is defined by symptoms, not by its cause.

ADHD is not alone among disorders that are not defined by cause. Autism, multiple sclerosis, and Parkinson's disease are examples of serious disorders known to be neurologically based but which have *no known* specific cause. In the case of autism it is possible that more than one biological event brings on the symptoms of the disorder. While the cause of Parkinson's disease remains unknown, there are clues that more than one cause triggers its onset: some toxins can bring on Parkinson's disease, and a high number of individuals exposed to the very severe flu epidemic of 1917 later developed Parkinson's disease. But of the many disorders that affect human behavior and development, only a few can be attributed to specific biological events.

Nevertheless, regardless of the ultimate cause, ADHD is thought to be associated with a disturbance in functioning of neurotransmitters in the brain.[1] Technological science is just beginning to reveal the role neurotransmitters play in ADHD. Neurotransmitters are natural body chemicals that transfer information from one brain cell to another. Neurotransmitters like dopamine, norepinephrine, and serotonin are now thought to occur at different levels among individuals who have hyperactivity than among those who have normal abilities to show sustained attention and arousal.[2] People with ADHD seem to have a reduced supply of these transmitters in areas of the brain that control attention and self-control.

We also know that some factors are associated—rightly or wrongly—with ADHD. We examine these factors below.

Factors Associated with ADHD

Over the years, certain potential causes of ADHD have come to light. That some of these factors cause ADHD has been borne out by research. Research has also shown that some things believed to cause ADHD in fact have no relation to the disorder.

We will review such possible causes as toxins affecting the fetus during pregnancy, toxins affecting the child after birth, accidents or traumas that affect the brain (producing ADHD-like symptoms), diet, and genetic factors.

As we review examples of "possible causes" of ADHD, it is important to keep in mind that in *most* cases children with ADHD got that way through no fault of the parents.

Toxins Affecting the Fetus During Pregnancy

It is now widely known that alcohol consumed during a pregnancy can cause a number of serious and long-term problems, including ADHD, to the child affected by such exposure. Fetal Alcohol Syndrome includes such effects as lowered intelligence, speech delays, poor fine-motor coordination, decreased attention span—ADHD—and other behavior problems.[3] As Fetal Alcohol Syndrome children enter adolescence and adulthood, they may show problems with judgment and memory. They likely have lower academic accomplishments compared to their age group, and they often have problems controlling anger. The effects of Fetal Alcohol Syndrome can also include microcephaly (small head size due to poor brain development) and changes in physical appearance.

Use of alcohol or other substances, such as heroin, methadone, and cocaine during pregnancy is now a leading cause of developmental disabilities. It is worth thinking about the fact that in our society we do little to prevent prenatal substance abuse, even though it is a leading cause of developmental problems among our children. We do not want to imply that most ADHD children became hyperactive because of prenatal exposure to alcohol or other drugs; however, we do report that use of alcohol, heroin, and the like can cause a multitude of serious problems including behavioral patterns common to ADHD.

Toxins Affecting the Child After Birth

Children are quite susceptible to lead poisoning. Lead poisoning in children can cause ADHD and learning disabilities.[4] At more serious levels of lead poisoning, the child may develop mental retardation and such other health problems as kidney and liver disorders. Extreme doses of lead in the body can be fatal.

Lead poisoning can be caused by a child chewing on furniture containing lead-based paint. Even breathing dust containing specks of lead-based paint can cause lead poisoning. Drinking water containing lead from improperly installed pipes with lead-based solder also can be a source of lead poisoning.

There is an objective laboratory blood test to determine if lead is a factor in a child's health problem. If lead is determined to be a factor, the source of the lead poisoning must be determined and removed. Once lead has caused damage to the brain, the damage may not be reversible.

Genetic Factors

A familial-genetic link can be associated with ADHD. This means that ADHD tends to occur in more than one member of a family and from one generation to another to a greater degree than would be expected merely by chance.[5] For example, if a person has a history of ADHD, then an offspring of that person would have a greater than normal chance of also having ADHD. (Normal expectation of problems in children is between 3 and 6 percent of the overall population.) Even parents who have no symptoms of ADHD may pass on ADHD traits to an offspring if other family members have ADHD or a learning disability that shows a familial genetic link.

There is evidence that genetic factors play a strong part in human behavior, including the development of ADHD. Some of the evidence is the following:

1. *Adoption studies*   A child whose biological parents have a family history of ADHD is at increased risk of developing ADHD, even if the adoptive parents have no history of ADHD. In contrast, a child whose biological parents did not have a family history of ADHD is not at increased risk of developing ADHD in an adoptive home. This kind of evidence from adoption studies suggests that an inherited risk from the biological parents had more to do with a child developing ADHD than the environment of the adoptive home.[6]
2. *Increased incidence of problems associated with ADHD occurring in siblings of ADHD children*   Problems associated with ADHD such as learning disabilities occur at a higher rate among siblings of an ADHD child than expected by chance. Dr. V. Gross-Tsur and colleagues studied all the children (6,950) who were born in Jerusalem in the year 1976. Nine years later about 3 percent of that group met the clinical criteria for ADHD.[5] That is within the range reported in the United States and other countries. Of the 145 children diagnosed as ADHD, a full 30 percent

had a sibling with a learning disability. The point is that if two disorders (e.g., ADHD and learning disability) often occur together in one family, a familial-genetic link is suggested, even if the two disorders do not occur in the same individual. The observed rate of learning disabilities among siblings of ADHD children was three times as high as would otherwise be expected.

3. *Sex differences* Boys around the world show rates of ADHD incidence about three times as high as girls.[7] There is reason to believe that boys may express the same genetic liability differently than girls: girls are more likely to express affective disorders such as depression and anxiety.

Accidents or Traumas That Affect the Brain

Injuries to the head are generally not associated with ADHD.

Henry Henry was seven years old when he was seriously injured in an auto accident. His injuries included a broken arm, multiple bruises and cuts, and a closed head injury (a head injury where the skull was not fractured). The head injury resulted in a coma that lasted two weeks. He developed swelling that caused pressure on the brain, and he needed brain surgery. Finally he regained consciousness, and his condition improved from critical to serious. He remained in the hospital for inpatient rehabilitation. He had difficulty with walking and with eye-hand coordination. He had speech difficulties as well as language and memory problems. While in the hospital he received rehabilitation therapy from a physical therapist, an occupational therapist, and a speech-language therapist.

When he returned home from the hospital, Henry had improved somewhat, but he was not his old self. He continued to need speech-language, physical, and occupational therapy. When he returned to school he needed extra help because it was harder for him to concentrate. He would leave his seat when it was inappropriate to do so, and he had major problems paying attention. School activities that had been easy for him before the accident were now difficult and caused him many frustrations. Poor eye-hand coordination made writing slow, labored, and inaccurate. He had difficulty with many areas of daily living that he had mastered before the accident. He needed assistance getting dressed, in part because of visual-spatial problems: for instance, he would put his shirt on back-ward—something he didn't do before the accident. He was more dependent on his parents and often became emotional and irritated when they helped him. In play with other children, he had problems with sharing and cooperation and became upset when another child had a favorite toy. His mother likened the emotionality of her seven-year, eight-month-old boy to that of a four-year-old.

Two years after the very serious accident Henry had substantially recovered but still needed special education services at school.

In many respects the problems encountered by Henry are very different from those described in this book about children with ADHD. While Henry did not recover completely, he did show substantial improvement as part of a recovery process and did so within a two-year period. In most cases of ADHD, cases not caused by a specific injury, the symptoms tend to be stable over time and do not show major resolution within a time frame as *brief* as two years.

MEDICAL PROCEDURES USED IN DIAGNOSIS AND TREATMENT

Henry suffered a specific brain injury and received specialized diagnostic tests to evaluate his neurologic status. These procedures included specialized medical evaluations to evaluate the brain such as computerized axial tomography (CAT) of the brain and electroencephalogram (EEG) studies. These specialized diagnostic procedures were important to his care and treatment. These specialized neurological procedures are not required or recommended in cases of ADHD that appear as a developmental pattern and not as a consequence of an injury.

DIAGNOSTIC STATEMENT

In the case of Henry, his medical chart listed problems that were stated as *secondary* to a traumatic injury that caused injury to his brain. His problem list included attention problems but also included motor coordination problems, expressive speech problems, and learning disability, all secondary to the head trauma.

Diet

Children who are malnourished or who skip breakfast or other meals are not as prepared as other children to play or learn. They become fatigued more easily than well-nourished children and do not concentrate as well on schoolwork. Good food is important for all children. Poor diet can lead to behavior and learning difficulties even in children who do not have ADHD.

THE FEINGOLD DIET

In 1973, Dr. Ben F. Feingold, an allergist, proposed that food additives such as salicylates, dyes, and preservatives caused allergic or toxic reactions in some children, which resulted in hyperactive behavior.[8] He reported dramatic behavioral improvements in hyperactive children placed on a diet free of salicylates and additives.[9] He was a popular speaker at meetings, and it was not uncommon for parents to give public testimonials to success stories about dramatic improvements of their children after being placed on the Feingold Diet. Many parents joined Feingold associations and altered their eating patterns to conform to the Feingold Diet. Even foods with naturally occurring salicylates, such as strawberries, oranges, peaches, and apples, were on the forbidden list. Some school programs changed their cafeteria foods so that salicylates, dyes, and additives were not present in the diet.

However, well-controlled studies using the double-blind research method have not supported the view that the Feingold Diet improves the behavior of hyperactive children.[10] In double-blind studies, neither the patient (the hyperactive child) nor the observer is aware of the treatment trials. An extensive review and summary of the Feingold Diet and ADHD was published in the *Journal of the American Medical Association* in 1982 as a report of the National Institutes of Health Consensus Development Panel.[11] The report concludes that the Feingold Diet may occasionally be effective for a very few hyperactive children. The great majority of hyperactive children were not improved by the Feingold Diet.

The current view is that diet management is not the treatment of choice for the great majority of hyperactive children. However, some infants and young children clearly show adverse reactions to some foods and the numbers of foods that can cause problematic reactions are much more extensive than suggested by Dr. Feingold.

THE BOCK STUDY

One important study has been reported by Dr. S. Allan Bock in *The Journal Pediatrics* in 1987. He studied 480 children from birth to age three. Of those children, 134 children, or 28 percent, were thought by their parents to have symptoms produced by certain foods.[12]

Dr. Bock's approach was different from Dr. Feingold's in several respects. First, he did not limit his study to dyes, salicylates, and food preservatives; he considered any food suspected by parents of possibly causing a reaction. He reports that virtually every food that might be eaten by an infant or young child was reported by at least one parent of the 480 children as having caused a reaction. His procedure then was to remove the suspected food until the symptoms disappeared. Then he employed either an "open challenge" of reintroducing the suspected food and waiting to observe a reaction or a "blind challenge," in which the ingredient of the suspected food was reformulated and hidden in other foods. If the blind challenge did not produce symptoms, the suspected food was presented openly to see if reactions developed. Which foods produced a reaction? The foods that caused or probably caused a reaction in at least one child of the 480 infants and young children in the study included fruits, fruit juices (such as tomato, orange, apple, and grape), milk, soy, peanut, egg, wheat, corn, and rice.

Adverse food reactions produced four kinds of symptoms:

1. *Gastrointestinal symptoms* Gastrointestinal symptoms were the most common and included diarrhea, vomiting, spitting, colic, and stomachaches.
2. *Skin reactions* Skin reactions included rashes.
3. *Respiratory reactions* Respiratory symptoms included nasal congestion, cough, and wheezing.
4. *Behavioral changes* Behavioral changes observed and reported consisted of increased restlessness and irritability.

A CLOSER LOOK AT BEHAVIOR CHANGES THAT RESULTED FROM FOOD REACTIONS

Some infants and young children did show behavioral symptoms—irritability and restlessess—caused by food reactions that at least look like early symptoms of ADHD. However, not one child showed behavioral problems only as a response to food reactions. Whenever a child showed a behavior reaction, the child *also* showed another reaction, such as a stomachache, diarrhea, vomiting, a skin reaction, nasal congestion, or wheezing. The child's behavioral change was most likely a direct response to discomfort from the symptoms of the food reaction.

An important feature of the Bock study was that when a food was confirmed to produce a reaction and was eliminated from the diet, the food would be reintroduced in small portions at regular intervals. In most cases as children grew they were able to tolerate foods that earlier in their development caused a reaction. This means that if a child once shows a reaction to a certain food, the food may not need to be eliminated permanently. By age three the great majority of children who showed adverse reactions as infants were able to eat those foods with no adverse symptoms.

It goes without saying that nutritious food is important for infants, children, and adults. It is also clear that infants and young children may show adverse reactions to some foods and that modification in diet—with occasional diet challenges—is prudent. We are aware of no carefully controlled study that shows that the Feingold Diet is an effective treatment for children with ADHD.

We also recognize that infants and young children, whether they have ADHD or not, may show adverse reactions to a wide variety of foods. It is helpful to know that the reactions are not exclusive to behavior and that symptoms such as diarrhea, vomiting, skin rash, or nasal congestion may be how a reaction is expressed. It is also helpful to know that in time foods that could not early on be tolerated may be safely reintroduced in the diet.

SUGAR AND ADHD

Research shows overwhelmingly that sugar does not cause hyperactivity. Dr. Mark Wolraich and associates (1986) carefully evaluated the food intake of both hyperactive and normal boys (those without ADHD). The consumpton of sugar averaged 15 percent of total energy consumed for both groups. The boys with ADHD did not consume more sugar than boys who were not hyperactive. Other studies have evaluated the behaviors of children after they have consumed food or soft drinks containing sugar. The results do not support a link between sugar and ADHD. It is true that parents and others have observed overactive behavior during such sugarfests as birthday parties and Halloween, but the behavior can be attributed to the emotional excitement of the event rather than the sugar consumed.

How Can I Be Certain of the Diagnosis of ADHD in My Child?

In this chapter we have discussed some causes of ADHD. These include toxins that affect a fetus during pregnancy and toxins that affect a child after birth. Injuries to the brain can cause problems including short attention span, overactivity, and impulsivity. For some, heredity may be the source of ADHD.

We indicated that for most children with ADHD, the exact cause may not be known. This raises an issue that often nags at parents: with uncertainty about cause of a condition, how certain can they be about the diagnosis?

If you have doubts about a diagnosis of ADHD, do raise questions. The following are examples of situations in which a parent would do well to doubt and question a suggested diagnosis of ADHD.

Your child shows behaviors of impulsivity, overactivity, and inattention, but it is out of character for him.

Mrs. Jones received a phone call from a teacher. The teacher reported that Mrs. Jones's son Erik was inattentive, often out of his seat, and not "tracking" in his third-grade class. The teacher suggested he might have ADHD.

Mrs. Jones remarked, "But we just moved. Everything has changed. We live in a new house. We are new in town. His nearest friend is a thousand miles away. Furthermore, he was a solid student his first two years in school."

Mrs. Jones has raised some excellent points. Her family had just moved, and such a major change in a child's environment can cause adjustment problems. Often problems associated with change in the family circumstances resolve themselves in time on their own.

Mrs. Jones also raised the question of duration of symptoms. If Mrs. Jones is correct that behavioral symptoms

were recent and lasted only a few months, then a diagnosis
of ADHD would be very suspect.

**You are told that a medical laboratory test such as an
EEG positively confirmed a diagnosis of ADHD in your
child.**

There is no brain-wave pattern measured by EEG equipment that is distinctive to ADHD. A laboratory test can
positively confirm a diagnosis of many disorders and diseases, but currently no laboratory test can positively confirm ADHD.

**Your physician or psychologist made a diagnosis of
ADHD based upon a brief interview with you, without
using standard behavioral rating scales and without
seeking independent information from your child's
teachers.**

You can be most certain about a diagnosis of ADHD if
the diagnostic process took time, as opposed to being made
in a quick one-shot evaluation. If information was gathered
from several settings, such as home and school, other possible causes were considered for the child's behavior, and
questions were taken seriously, then the diagnosis of
ADHD is likely to be more reliable.

---

*A multidisciplinary team evaluation is the safest and most de-
pendable way to determine if your child is ADHD.*

CHAPTER 3

Who Should Evaluate Your Child?: Working with Professionals

Now that you know the importance of a complete and thorough evaluation for your child, your next question may well be: "Who should evaluate my child, and how do I find qualified people?" You should start with your own local doctor. The local pediatrician will want to do some preliminary screening to rule out physical problems that can cause attention problems. He will want to do standard vision and hearing tests and refer to specialists if needed: an ophthalmologist for vision problems and an audiologist or an ENT (ear, nose and throat) doctor if hearing problems are involved. If nothing is found, the pediatrician will move on to the next step.

At this point the local pediatrician may do one of two things: he may refer you, either to a team or to a more specialized physician, such as a developmental pediatrician (a pediatrician specializing in how children develop mentally and physically), a child psychiatrist, a pediatric neurologist, or a behavioral pediatrician (a pediatrician specializing in childhood behavior); or he may just say, "Your child is hyperactive. We'll put him on Ritalin."

If your pediatrician does the latter, stay calm. He may be a very good pediatrician, but he needs an educational update on ADHD. All you need to do is be honest with him:

> Dr. Jones, I don't feel very comfortable putting Bobby on Ritalin until we've looked into learning disabilities and

some other possible causes of his attention problems. I know that a lot of hyperactive children have learning disabilities as well. If he is hyperactive, I'm concerned that he may have learning disabilities, too, and I know how important it is to identify the strengths and weaknesses of any child with attention problems. Could I please have a referral to a team that includes a learning disabilities specialist and a child psychologist?

Your doctor may say, "Okay, but why don't we go ahead and try the medication? That may solve all of your problems, and you might find out Bobby doesn't have any problems in school after we start the medication."

He could be right. Your child could be one of the lucky children with ADHD who has no other problems, but on the other hand, something else could be causing his attention problems and he may not even need medication. You could be wasting valuable time if you just wait to find that out. ADHD can be mild, moderate, or severe, and it is important to know just what you're dealing with. Likewise, it requires some special techniques in school and at home, techniques that are taught best by specialists who have examined the child. Stress that point to your doctor and tell him you really would like an evaluation of your child that includes a learning assessment and a psychological assessment so you know what your child's strengths and weaknesses are and the best way to work with him.

Most doctors will not be the least offended if you handle it that smoothly. Remember, you are both on the same side, and he cares about your child, too. Most pediatricians are very aware that learning disabilities and behavior problems are common problems associated with ADHD, and they, too, will want a team assessment done on your child.

In all likelihood, your doctor will know of a multidisciplinary team somewhere in your state. We have listed some in Appendix C of this book. University medical schools often have pediatric departments or child development labs connected with them, and they are an excellent source of good diagnostic teams. If none of them are close to you, by all means call the American Academy of Pediatrics or Physician's Referral and ask for a referral to either a developmental pediatrician or a child psychiatrist. Both developmental pediatricians and child psychiatrists and child psychologists have a lot of experience with hyperactive children. There is a good chance they work with learning disabilities specialists and other specialists in either a formal team or informal team format. Keep in mind that your insurance may dictate your choice of doctors.

What If I Live in a Small Town?

It may be fairly easy to find an established team if you live in a city, but in a small town you may be lucky to find a pediatrician. If you can only find one of these specialists in your area, you may have to put together your own team. Start with professionals located in your area. If you have found a good child psychologist, he may know a pediatrician he has worked with who is knowledgeable about ADHD. Then you may need to add a learning disabilities specialist to the team. Most child psychologists will know one or more LD specialists. You now have a core team put together. Ask the pediatrician and the child psychologist if they can run the kinds of tests we discuss in chapters 1 and 3 of this book (that is, neurodevelopmental, speech and hearing, Learning Disabilities and psychological tests). From that point on, the pediatrician and the child psychologist will have to lead you to other experts as required by your child's specific needs. To form a team you will want to bring together the child psychologist, the pediatrician, the learning disabilities specialist, and your child's teacher, as well as any other specialists needed. You will have to arrange a mutually convenient time and place for them to meet, maybe the pediatrician's office after school. The professionals and the pediatrician will then team up to evaluate all areas of your child's life.

In coming together, professionals and parents share information, insights, and test results. Most important, the professionals and you can share ideas on what can and should be done for your child to help him at school and at home. Some of the members of the initial evaluating team may stay on as part of the ongoing management team. The ongoing management team almost always consists of parents, teacher, child psychologist, and pediatrician.

You may wonder how you can tell if the team evaluating your child is a good one. If you know and trust your doctor, then that is where you begin, but you should ask around also. We have listed some support groups in Appendix E and you can ask other parents at the support groups. Hopefully, those you have asked for recommendations will base their assessments of a team's quality on the thoroughness of the team. You can call the child development department at your local university and ask to speak to someone who can recommend a team. Another source to question is your school district. School districts will sometimes call upon a diagnostic team for complicated cases. And besides asking around, you can get a fair idea of a team's quality by looking at their experience, and the thoroughness of their work.

Some school districts may even have their own diagnostic team. Parents should be very careful of diagnostic teams run by the schools. While people in the educational system generally know a great deal about learning disabilities, they are often woefully lacking in knowledge of child development, neurology, and specialized areas of child psychology. Parents should always ask, "Who will be on the team? What are their credentials? Is there a developmental pediatrician or neurologist? Is the psycholgist a Ph.D. in child psychology?" Be aware that school districts often have a "school psychologist" whose qualifications may be less than you expected. Instead of a Ph.D., the educational qualification might be only an M.S. in educational psychology. While the school psychologists may have many courses in counseling and testing, they may have little coursework in child development and child psychology, and none in neurology.

In many states a school psychologist can be a teacher with additional courses in educational psychology. That is a far cry from a clinical psychologist with a Ph.D. and a subspecialty in child psychology. These are questions you should ask regardless of which team you select. Remember, you need a thorough diagnosis done by highly qualified people who can interpret the findings and offer solid suggestions for helping your child improve at school and at home.

Who Should Be on the Team?

An evaluation team can consist of as few as two people, usually a developmental pediatrician and a child psychologist, or as many as five or six people. If there is an indication that the child has learning disabilities, then there should always be a learning disabilities specialist. Other specialists we see on teams are neurologists, physical therapists, speech therapists, social workers, and behavioral pediatricians. Who will be on the team to assess *your* child will depend entirely on the needs of the child. For instance, if your child did not talk until he was three and did not walk until he was two, the team must have a speech therapist and a physical therapist. Of course you would also need a developmental pediatrician and a child psychologist as well. If your child is a foster child and has been in another home before he came to live with you, you might also request a social worker.

Aspects of a Thorough Evaluation

At a thorough screening for ADHD, doctors will look at all areas of the child's life. While this is time-consuming, it gives the clearest picture of the child, highlighting both the child's weaknesses and his strengths. Looking at the child's environment (home, school, baby-sitters) also can reveal stress factors that may contribute to the problem. And whether or not the problem turns out to be ADHD, the probable cause or causes of the problem may be discovered.

Medical History

You can expect doctors to want a complete medical history. They will want to know about the pregnancy. Were there any problems in the pregnancy or at delivery? They will also want to know if your child takes any medications, such as theophylline (which can cause jittery behavior or inability to concentrate) for asthma, or phenobarbital (which can cause overactivity) for epilepsy. They will want to know if your child has had any head injuries or other serious medical problems.

You should tell them of any drugs the child's mother took, or medications prescribed or over-the-counter, during pregnancy. Doctors need to know if the mother took even moderate amounts of alcohol or other psychoactive drugs during pregnancy.

There are some other questions doctors may ask. Does the child have metabolic problems, such as phenylketonuria (PKU), or has there been lead poisoning or an ongoing illness? Has he had congenital heart disease leading to hypoxia (low oxygen levels in the blood), or has his heart ever stopped and been revived? They will want to know about any of the following conditions as well:

under- or overactive thyroid
recurrent diabetic problems
diabetic coma
hypoglycemia (low blood sugar)
ongoing anemia
food allergies

If you kept a baby book or other records of your child's growth and development, bring it along to your appointment, because an assessment team will always ask for a developmental history of your child. When did he sit up, walk, say his first words? Knowing the answers to all of the above questions helps the evaluation team to obtain the clearest possible picture of your child's medical history.

Family History

A family history tells about the blood relatives of the child and the types of problems in the family. Are there any allergies, autoimmune diseases, seizure disorders, learning problems, or instances of retardation? What kinds of jobs do family members have, and how much education do they have? Have other family members had problems in school, had learning problems, or had attention problems? Has there been drug abuse or depression? Has anyone had to repeat one or more grades?

Doctors will want to know if other people in your family are also hyperactive. Was either parent hyperactive as a child? Were any of the grandparents hyperactive? Are any of your other children ADHD? While there is not a specific chromosomal pattern that causes ADHD, we do know there is a genetic link in 30 to 40 percent of the cases.

Social History

The evaluation team will ask about the child's social history. Have there been changes in the child's life that could cause behavior problems? Has there been a divorce, a move away from close family members, or other problems? If the parents are separated, is one parent the "fun" parent, while the other parent is "the wicked witch of the west"? Do stepparents understand this child's problems, or do they see him as a "spoiled child"? Do the parents have realistic expectations for the child? Does Dad see his frail, underweight son becoming a professional football player or Mom see her C student becoming a doctor?

Temperament

As we said in Chapter 1, temperament is something that must be considered. What the team will look for is a match or mismatch between the child and his environment. They will want to see if there is a "goodness of fit" in the home and at school.[1] Some children have trouble adapting to certain situations and settings. A child who is a real mover and shaker may have trouble with a teacher who likes everything very quiet and orderly. High-energy children may have trouble fitting into a family where everyone else is laid-back and easygoing. Incompatibility between the environment and the child's intrinsic behavioral style can cause problems, but the problem is not the temperament itself.

Thomas and Chess[2] described nine components of temperament in their twelve-year study. The following are their components of temperament:

Activity level the proportion of active periods to inactive periods

Rhythmicity the regularity of hunger, excretion, sleep, and wakefulness

Distractibility the degree to which extraneous stimuli change behavior

Approach/withdrawal the initial response to new objects or people, which can be positive or negative

Adaptability the ease with which a child adapts to change in the environment

Attention span/persistence the amount of time devoted to one activity and the effect of distraction on the activity

Intensity of reaction the energy of response, regardless of its quality or direction

Threshold of responsiveness the intensity of stimulation required to evoke a response

Quality of mood the amount of friendly, pleasant, joyful

behavior as contrasted with unfriendly, unpleasant, and unhappy behavior

While temperamental characteristics appear to be genetically determined, they may be modified by interaction with physical
and environmental factors. Children may fall into one of three
temperamental types (easy child, slow-to-warm-up child, and
difficult child) based upon ratings of high or low in each of the
nine categories. Temperamental characteristics are important because children with a higher score in activity levels, distractibility,
or attention span/persistence are easily mistaken for hyperactive
children, when this could be a normal variation of temperament.
Children with "difficult" temperaments may share those
symptoms with hyperactive children, but the "difficult" child is
different because his overactivity may be fairly organized and
purposeful.

Physical Condition

For the most part, doctors will do a physical exam that is not
very different from an extensive "back-to-school" type exam.
They will do all of the standard things we mentioned before,
and look for medical problems that could possibly affect behavior: Speech and hearing problems, visual difficulty, neurological disorders like muscular dystrophy, evidence of any minor
seizures, heart disease (which could cause low oxygen levels and
even anemia), hypoglycemia, and food allergies. Most children
with ADHD have very normal physical and standard neurological exams.

Examiners may do a neurodevelopmental exam. This exam
may differ from other exams your child has had only because
the doctors will want to do a neurodevelopmental exam to see
how your child's central nervous system and sensory systems
are developing. They will want to compare your child's development with that of "normal" children. This is important because sometimes children are misdiagnosed as "hyperactive"
when they have other neurodevelopmental delays.

For a neurodevelopmental exam you can expect the team to give your child a series of tasks designed to test the following:

- coordination
- memory
- ability to put things in sequence
- fine-motor skills
- ability to remember a number of commands

School Functioning

Another area the team will want to look at is how well your child is doing in school. Many times the child is referred to the team by the school because he is impulsive and "doesn't pay attention." The doctors will send forms to the school ahead of time. These forms ask questions about your child's behavior in the classroom: Does he follow directions? Does he wait for his turn? Does he finish his work? Does he daydream? Does he stay on-task?

Teams also consider the type of school setting the child is in, the size of the school, and whether or not special help is available. The team will ask all of these questions and give both the school and the parents some of the more common standardized rating forms as well. Behavioral checklists were developed by careful study of observations by and concerns of parents and teachers about the child's behavior. The checklists provide a standard way for parents and teachers to state their views of how a child behaves. The items in these scales include, but are not limited to, behaviors associated with ADHD. These forms include the following:

Achenbach Child Behavior Rating Scales   The Achenbach scales call for a record of the child's involvement in activities such as sports, hobbies, clubs, chores, friendships, and school. The parents' form includes a list of 113 behavioral, social, and emotional problems.

Barkley's Home and School Social Questionnaires   These

were developed by Dr. Russell Barkley to evaluate the situations—both at home and in school—that are difficult for children. They focus on the situations that are difficult rather than how the child misbehaves.

Conners Rating Scales (Teacher's Questionnaire and Parent's Questionnaire) The Conners scales cover a range of behavior problems, including items associated with ADHD.

Vineland Adaptive Scales These are used in an interview format. The parents are asked to describe skills shown by their child in areas of self-care, communication, responsibility, social skills, and judgment in handling money.

The questionnaires are broken down into age groups of three to five, six to eleven, and twelve or older. The reason parents are asked about their child's behavior at school is because children will often tell parents things they have not told their teacher. Remember, the team wants to see all sides of the child to get a full understanding of his behavior. There is another questionnaire, the Anser Form, that asks not only parents and teachers, but also the child (if he is nine or older), about his behavior.

School questionnaires ask teachers for descriptions of the child's school difficulties and strengths. Teachers rate the child's performance in reading, writing, spelling, general knowledge, mathematics, oral expression, ability to complete work/activities, efficiency, and preparation for daily class. The child is rated as strong, average, somewhat deficient, or markedly deficient in comparison to his classmates. The child is also rated on humor, creativity, enthusiasm for learning, and extracurricular activities. These forms also ask questions designed to pick up on depression in children, so the child can be referred to a child psychologist if need be.

Emotional Condition

Children with emotional problems also can appear to be hyperactive. Through interviews with the family and the child, a skilled child psychologist will look for such problems as anxiety, phobia, oppositional behavior, anger, sadness, depression, child abuse, bizarre behavior, autism, and psychotic disorders. If emotional problems are at the root of the hyperactive behavior, therapy may well correct what looked like hyperactivity on the surface.

Learning Disabilities

There is one other area that a team must look at: learning disabilities. Many hyperactive children also have additional learning disabilities. Some children have learning disabilities and *do not have* ADHD; however, inattention and overactivity caused by the learning disability may make a child's family or teachers think he is hyperactive. A good diagnostic team will be able to use specific kinds of testing to separate abilities and disabilities. They may look for learning disabilities in some of the following areas:

perception (visual or auditory or both)
listening comprehension
basic reading skills
reading comprehension
memory (both short-term and experiential)
sequencing
oral expression
written expression
spelling
math calculation
math reasoning
fine-motor skills (in handwriting or other skills)

Psychologists will also want to look at learning style as well. How does your child learn? Does he learn by listening, by looking, or only by actually doing or participating? Knowing that learning disabilities can masquerade as hyperactivity and that children—whether or not they have learning problems— have different styles of learning makes the importance of thorough testing obvious.

Narrowing the Focus of the Investigation

When it is decided that a child has trouble with attention, doctors may decide to look at what area or areas are affected in your child. Attention can be broken down into the following seven components:[3]

- *State of Arousal*   A person's state of arousal is his alertness, and it varies in each individual. Some people do their best work in the morning, while others work best in the evening. State of arousal is related to brain function and perhaps is involved with transferring signals from one part of the brain to the other. Some doctors think that the state of arousal is related to the function of neurotransmitters. Brain cells called neurons pass information from one cell to the next using the brain chemicals we call neurotransmitters. Neurotransmitters are affected by stimulants (like Ritalin or even caffeine), or they can be altered by sedatives.
- *Impulsivity/Reflectivity*   Everyone has a balance between impulsivity and reflectivity (or how long you *think* about something before you do it). Does the child like to do things quickly, or does he like to take his time and study situations from many angles? There are situations where a quick response is appropriate (flash cards, Nintendo, an emergency) and other situations that require a reflective style (drawing a picture, writing a story). Individuals may be better at dealing with one kind of situation than another.
- *Cognitive Tempo*   Cognitive tempo is the speed with

which you *do* a task. Some people work rapidly whereas others move slowly and take their time doing things.

- *Filtering of Distractions* Even though some children can listen to the teacher, they have trouble filtering out the noise of other children on the playground or the class next door.
- *Purposeful Focus* Some people have trouble focusing their attention. Purposeful focus is the ability to select and focus on what is important. They may not be able to keep their attention on the teacher with other things going on (teacher is giving a reading lesson, Bobby is pulling Shannon's hair, Meg is doodling on her work sheet). The ability to select and focus attention is important to success in doing tasks.
- *Vigilance* Vigilance is the length of time you can pay attention to the task at hand. It requires making moment-by-moment choices of where to focus your attention. It requires constant sharpening and refining of attention, while the quality of attention is assured by self-monitoring.
- *Self-monitoring* Self-monitoring is the quality control of attention. It is what makes sure that you are reading a book instead of daydreaming. Monitoring, especially in boring tasks, maintains the quality of attention necessary to read a book and understand what you have read.

You can see why having trouble with any one of the areas of attention we have discussed would make learning difficult for your child. Different areas of difficulty in attention may require different solutions in the classroom or at home. If your child has trouble with vigilance, then doing work on the computer, with constant feedback, will help. Your child will do better if he has his hardest classes when he is most alert, and children who have difficulty with alertness will do better with animated, vivacious teachers. Sitting closer to the teacher's desk may help children with problems focusing attention. Knowing what areas of attention are difficult for your child will allow the team to make suggestions about the best ways to overcome areas of difficulty.

After the Testing: What to Do with the Results

It is very difficult for parents to interpret the results from these tests. Someone from the team, usually the child psychologist, will sit down with you and go over the team's findings. In its report, the team will offer suggestions for things you can do at home and recommendations for things the school can do to help your child. Usually the team recommends a course of action that may include setting up a management team of a child psychologist, the pediatrician, the child's teacher, and you, his parents. Based on its findings, the team may or may not recommend that you try medication for your child. The team will want to hear from you as well, so ask questions' and express your concerns, even if you think they may sound stupid.

You can ask for a copy of the results for your own files, and a copy will surely be sent to your child's school with your permission. In all probability, the team will also set up an appointment with the school when you can be present and will go over the same information with the school. The team will make recommendations to you and to the school on strategies for teaching your child.

When you consider all the areas that should be looked into and all of the possibilities that must be considered, it is easy to see why a team assessment is preferable to the opinion of one professional. But what if you only have one doctor in your small town and he knows little about hyperactivity other than to prescribe Ritalin? What should you do? How far should you go with him?

Follow the recommendations we made earlier when we talked about where to begin. The most important thing to remember is to deal honestly and openly with your doctor. Talk to him. All too often patients do not like what a doctor says and leave the doctor altogether, instead of having an open discussion with him. Tell the doctor what your concerns are. Tell him why you are concerned. Then listen to him. Listen to his explanations and what he wants you to know. Always ask questions. Most doctors will answer them gladly, though a few will not. Remember that you and your doctor both have personalities, too. He may not have the time for or the interest in treating cases like ADHD. These cases take a lot of the doctor's time, and they are not curable. The doctor may not like working with these kinds of problems. Ask your doctor if he is interested in working with a child management team composed of you, your child, the school, a child psychologist, and of course a pediatrician.

If your doctor is not interested in working with the team or if you think he would not work well with the management team, what should you do?

Here again, be honest. "Dr. Jones, I have decided to have a multidisciplinary team evaluate Billy. Would you please transfer Billy's records to Dr. Smith? Dr. Smith is part of the team we have decided to use. Thank you for all you have done for Billy."

Legally, you have the right to a copy of all medical records. People change doctors all the time, and their office staffs are used to transferring records.

CHAPTER 4

The Use of Ritalin and Other Medications in the Treatment of ADHD

Parents of a child with ADHD come to realize that hyperactivity is not a passing phase of overactivity and inattention. The symptoms normally last for years and for many extend into adulthood. Children with ADHD cannot just "pull themselves together."

In this chapter we will review the use of medication as part of a treatment plan for children who have ADHD. We will also discuss the pros and cons of medication in the treatment of hyperactivity, the types of medication, dosages, long-term effects, side effects, and ways of monitoring effects. Finally, we will discuss how long a child with ADHD may need to be on medication.

Helping Your Child with ADHD

One of the most important things you can do as a parent of a child with ADHD is get an accurate diagnosis and an appropriate treatment plan. As you have learned, all children may show indications of emotional overresponsiveness, inattention, and overactivity from time to time. However, it is the persistence of the symptoms over time and in many situations that is important in the diagnosis of ADHD. Furthermore, it is important

49

for us to rule out or consider a number of issues that may cause a child to be overactive, to act impulsively, and to be distractible before making a diagnosis of ADHD. These issues are discussed in Chapters 1 and 2.

How Effective Is Treatment of ADHD?

Over 75 percent of children with ADHD can be helped with medication. We wish we could say it is 100 percent as it is with current treatment programs for PKU. ADHD is the most common childhood mental disorder, so the fact that as many as 75 percent of children with ADHD can show a positive response to treatment (medication and behavior management) is important. That figure is in the same range as treatment success for depression, the most common adult mental disorder. It is our belief that most children with ADHD can live successful, productive lives with appropriate diagnosis and a broad-based treatment plan.

Why Medication at All in the Treatment of ADHD?

ADHD, or hyperactivity, is a disorder that can be caused by many conditions. Regardless of the ultimate cause, ADHD is thought to be associated with a disturbance in the functioning of neurotransmitters in the brain.[1] Neurotransmitters are natural body chemicals that transfer information from one brain cell to another. Neurotransmitters like dopamine, norepinephrine, and serotonin are now thought to be present at different levels in the brains of individuals who have hyperactivity as compared to others who have normal abilities to show sustained attention and stay alert. People with ADHD seem to have a decreased supply of these transmitters in areas of the brain that control attention and self-control. Medications to treat hyperactivity appear to increase arousal and alertness of the brain by increasing the supply of chemical neurotransmitters like dopamine, norepinephrine, and serotonin. These neurotransmitters help information move from one brain cell to another.

Many parents ask *why would anyone give a stimulant to children who are already overactive and impulsive?* When we use the word *stimulant* as applied to medications such as Ritalin, Cylert, and Dexedrine, we mean that they stimulate neurotransmitters in the brain, like dopamine, to help the brain work better. The word *stimulant* when applied to these medications is not meant to imply that they stimulate children to make them more active. For a long time most people thought that hyperactive children had a paradoxical or opposite reaction to stimulants. We know that by stimulating neurotransmitters in the brain these medications help an overactive child become less active. People with hyperactivity have the same reaction to stimulants that "normal" people do; however, the improvements for people with ADHD are indeed more dramatic than they are for "normal" people.[2]

Ritalin alone is not a magic pill. It cannot cure a child with ADHD like penicillin can cure an ear infection. Medications are usually *not* sufficient in themselves to solve the many problems associated with hyperactivity. However, stimulant medications can be an important part of a treatment program and should be used *with* behavioral management therapy and any other remedial educational programs needed.

The main treatment effects of the stimulants (Ritalin, Dexedrine, and Cylert) are as follows:

1. Improve attention span
2. Reduce impulsive behavior
3. Reduce disruptive behavior
4. Increase compliant behavior

Parents also report that they can manage their child's behavior with fewer reprimands and punishments.

The most commonly used stimulants to treat ADHD are Ritalin (methylphenidate), Dexedrine (dextroamphetamine), and Cylert (pemoline). Ritalin is used most often because of its safety record, even for younger children. Dexedrine is a stronger medication, and Cylert is reserved for older, school-aged children. Ritalin and Dexedrine are fast-acting medications that usually show some response within about forty minutes of taking the medication. In both cases the benefits of the medication wear off after about four hours. In most cases children taking Ritalin or Dexedrine take the medication twice a day, once in the morning and again about noon. Usually the effects of the medication are gone by the time a school-age child has returned home from school.

Dosages are measured throughout the world on the metric system and determined by milligrams of medication per kilogram of body weight. Usual dosage of Ritalin is in the range of 0.3 to 0.7 milligrams per kilogram of body weight. Usual dosage of Dexedrine is in the range of 0.15 to 0.4 milligrams per kilogram of body weight. Some physicians use set dosages of 5 mg, 10 mg, 15 mg, and 20 mg of medication instead of calculating for body weight. Dosages must be individualized, based on response to the medication—be it low or high dose.

Cylert or pemoline is a longer-lasting medication than either Ritalin or Dexedrine. Cylert is given one time a day, and after a few days, the effect is fairly steady. Additionally, there is a sustained-release form of Ritalin that maintains its effect for eight to twelve hours. This can be an advantage to some children who find it embarrassing or inconvenient to take a second pill during the day.

Should Your Child Take Ritalin or Any Stimulant Medication for ADHD?

The Issue of Age and the Use of Medication

If you are sure that your child has been appropriately diagnosed with ADHD, the use of Ritalin or one of the other medications could well be an important part of a treatment program.

AGE AND MEDICATION

In most cases placing a very young child on Ritalin or the other stimulant medications is a last-resort decision. Apart from problems of diagnosing ADHD in a three-year-old, stimulant medications are usually not as effective before age five. Preschool children usually respond better to behavioral management strategies than to medication, but there are exceptions.

Even for young children for whom a diagnosis of ADHD is very compelling and certain, stimulants may not work well. If stimulants are used and are not effective, the parents may not be willing to try them again when the child is older and his central nervous system has matured to the point where the medications may be helpful.

Once a Child Is Placed on a Medication for ADHD, How Long Will the Child Continue to Take This Medication?

Whereas most children who are placed on a stimulant medication continue to take the medication right on through adolescence and into the teenage years, children with mild ADHD may need medication for only a few years or until they develop strategies to cope with the related problems. ADHD is a chronic (or long-term) condition. If medication works, in all likelihood it will need to be taken for many years. However, as a person with ADHD matures, response to medication changes. Some may need less medication during their teen years. Few individuals with ADHD take a stimulant medication like Ritalin after twenty years of age. For those who continue to need a medication in their teen years, a shift to a tricyclic antidepressant (such as Desipramine) may prove helpful. This is not to imply a hard and fast rule but is meant to emphasize the fact that as a child with ADHD grows and matures his response to a medication may change. Furthermore, how long the medication is needed depends on the individual child and his ability to cope with his ADHD.

Pros and Cons of Stimulant Medication in the Treatment of ADHD

Ritalin and other stimulant medications have been among the most widely studied drugs for the last forty years. The safety of the medication, when properly prescribed and used, is not really the question. Rather the question is: should medication be used in every case of inattention?

In chapter 1 we saw examples of children who had attention problems that were helped by means other than medication. While Ritalin in itself is safe, it can be abused by teachers who are anxious to "help" overactive children sit down and pay attention or by doctors who, in an effort to cooperate with parents or teachers, prescribe the drug too quickly, without looking into possible causes for the inattention.

Not every child with attention problems should be on medication. Children with mild ADHD may not need medication. Children who respond very well to behavior management therapy alone may not need medication. The decision to use medication should be made by parents, physician, and psychologist, with input from the teacher. Parents who feel uncomfortable with medication may want to check and see if their child can do without it. Make the decision with your team, considering all of the potential advantages and disadvantages for your child.

The main advantage of stimulant medication is that it can help a child be more focused and attentive and reduce overactive and disruptive behavior. The main disadvantages are side effects and the short-term behavioral effects of the medication. For most children with ADHD, when the school day is over the effects of stimulant medication are over as well. Parents are usually left with the brunt of problems associated with ADHD. This is not to discourage the use of stimulant medication but to place its use in perspective.

Why Is It Bad to Give a Child Medication Throughout the Day?

Pediatricians recognize that stimulant medications such as Ritalin may reduce a child's appetite if given within an hour of a major meal or may cause a child to sleep poorly if given too late in the afternoon. Medication should last through homework and wear off at bedtime. A decision to use medication in late afternoon and early evening should be determined by a review of the child's behavior and possible side effects of the stimulant medication.

How Can One Monitor the Usefulness of Stimulant Medications?

There are three issues to consider in evaluating the effects of stimulant medication for appropriately diagnosed children with ADHD. They are as follows:

1. Is the medication effective?
2. Are there lasting side effects of the medication that are troublesome and outweigh the advantage of the medication?
3. If medication is effective, is one dosage level better than another?
4. Has it improved school performance?

The Effectiveness of Medication in the Treatment of ADHD

The most accurate and, frankly, the simplest procedure to tell if a stimulant medication is effective for a child is recording of observations and impressions in the form of behavior ratings. It is also important to have teachers' ratings to see if the behavior of the child at school has shown improvement. We recommend the Conners Rating Scales, which have one version for parents and another for teachers. As the child gets older, he, too, should be asked questions about his behavior and school performance, both on and off medication.

The Conners Rating Scales are easy to read and complete. The rating scales list problems known to be associated with ADHD and ask that a parent or teacher indicate the degree of the problem by a check mark. One question is illustrated below:

	Not at all	Just a little	Pretty much	Very much
Restless in the squirmy sense				

It is a good idea to have some baseline rating for a week or so before a child is placed on stimulant medications, as well as ratings for at least three to four weeks after a child has been placed on medication.

Some parents are surprised that behavior ratings compiled by themselves and by teachers are the main method used to evaluate medications for ADHD. However, blood studies, laboratory studies, and neurological exams are not as helpful in evaluating the effectiveness of medications as behavior ratings by people who live with, work with, or teach the children.

There are psychological laboratory procedures such as the Kagan Matching Familiar Figures or the Gordon Test of Vigilance that are used in evaluating improvement in the attention span of children with ADHD. Neither should be used *instead* of behavior rating scales, but both can be used as supplements. Both tests require a child to attend to stimuli before responding, and ADHD children as a group do not perform as well as non-ADHD children. However, since the tests are administered individually, a procedure that aids the performance of the ADHD child, the contrast in performance of ADHD children and normal children is not as great as what would be observed by an experienced teacher in a classroom setting.

The Question of Side Effects

It is important in considering the use of stimulant medications to look for possible unwanted side effects. The issue of safety of any medication is whether the risk of unwanted side effects is judged acceptable or not, in light of the good that may be gained by its use.

Stimulant medications for the treatment of children with ADHD are considered safe. However, some side effects have been reported.[3] We list problems that have been reported below.

POSSIBLE SIDE EFFECTS OF STIMULANT MEDICATIONS

1. Difficulty sleeping
2. Stares or daydreams
3. Lack of interest in activities
4. Decreased appetite
5. Increased irritability
6. Body complaints such as stomachaches, headaches, or dizziness
7. Increased crying or signs of anxiety
8. Increased blood pressure and heart rate

About one child in a hundred develops tics (involuntary motor and vocal spasms) after receiving Ritalin. If this occurs, consult your local physician immediately, and it is likely the medication will be discontinued or changed. Your doctor may recommend another medication or a treatment program without medication.

Children with a family history of tics or Tourette's Syndrome usually should not be given Ritalin or other stimulants. If you have a history of tics or Tourette's be sure to tell your physician *before* he prescribes a stimulant for your child.

If you feel your child is depressed, anxious, or withdrawn, be sure to tell your physician. Stimulant medications may make these conditions worse, and other medications should be used instead. Tofranil (imipramine hydrochloride) is an example of a medication that is used for affective disorders such as depression or anxiety that has also proved helpful for some ADHD children.

Most side effects of stimulant medications are not serious and occur early in treatment, so parents should not be discouraged if their child with hyperactivity does not respond to treatment immediately and shows troublesome side effects like weight loss during initial treatment.

Do record your observations in the form of behavior ratings and request your child's teacher to do the same. Review them with your child's physician or with a psychologist.

Dosage Levels of Medication

If your child has been on medication for a while and he has grown over time through normal development, remember that the medication is given in terms of milligrams per kilogram of weight. If your child was started on medication when he weighed forty-four pounds (twenty kilos) and now weighs sixty-six pounds (thirty kilos), the dosage of medication may need to be adjusted. It is helpful to repeat a series of behavior ratings several times a week at home and at school over a six-to-eight-week period to see if a child shows improvement after a change in amount of medication.

Stimulant medications are not addictive, so you need not be

concerned about that issue. Stimulant medications also do not cause a person to take illegal street drugs. There may be a problem if stimulant medication is taken in combination with other medications. If your child is taking a medication of any type, review it with your physician to see if it may create a problem if a stimulant medication is being considered.

Living with ADHD
in the Home

CHAPTER 5

Organizing the Environment

Part 1 of this book was designed to help you understand attention problems and ADHD as well as the medications used to treat them. Hopefully, you and your team have sat down with your child and decided whether or not to use medication. Regardless of how that decision turned out, our team would like you to know medication is only part of the answer. The authors of this book feel that medication should be used in conjunction with behavior management techniques. If you and your team decided *not* to use medication, then behavior management is crucial. Part 2 of this book explains management techniques, and it is designed to help you live with ADHD.

Whether this is your first book about hyperactive children or your twentieth, every book will tell you that your hyperactive child needs a *structured environment*. You may be wondering what exactly a structured environment is, how parents create one, and why hyperactive children need it so badly.

An educational psychology textbook once defined structure as: setting limits, rewarding and giving consequences for behavior, controlling and directing, manipulating and organizing, scheduling and maintaining standards for behavior.[1] Two elements, control and direction, have the potential to cause problems for a child when misused by adults who see that their child is out of control. Mom, Dad, or teacher may long to see the child exercise some self-control, and when he does not, they find themselves exercising too much control or overdirecting the child. So, how do we have structure without using too much control or overdirecting the child? Remember, you want to structure the environment, not the child. Both control and direction are things you do to the child, while everything else in that definition can be done to the child's environment, thereby structuring the environment.

Structure is order, organization, and predictability. For most of us, structure is something we do automatically with our environment: we put things in order, we organize them so we can predict where they will be found, and by doing so we can work more efficiently. Hyperactive children have great difficulty organizing or ordering their environment.

Throughout this book you will find we use the same systems repeatedly to help children organize:

breaking down tasks into their fewest basic steps
setting priorities
structuring or organizing the environment
organizing time
pairing as many stimuli as possible (visual, auditory, tactile, et cetera)
feedback in the form of praise and rewards

Breaking Down Tasks into Their Fewest Basic Steps

Everything we do is done in a series of steps. You can look at any job and break it down into steps. Washing dishes requires many steps: collecting the dishes from the table, scraping food from plates, rinsing dishes, washing in hot, soapy water, rinsing in clean water, drying, and putting away. If you have a dishwasher, you can eliminate some of the last steps, but you will also want to find a way of eliminating the first two. Having each family member bring his own plate to the counter and scrape it eliminates the first two steps and makes a two-step job of rinsing and putting dishes in the dishwasher a manageable job for the ADHD child. It is best to eliminate any unnecessary steps, so that the task will require the child's attention for a much shorter time and there will be fewer steps where a child can fail.

Making a bed is another example. By putting just a comforter on your child's bed you can eliminate a top sheet and a bedspread, thus vastly simplifying the child's task.

Cleaning a room is made easier by placing a row of hooks in a closet to hang pajamas and play clothes on and by using plastic bins or cardboard boxes for toys with lots of little parts, like Lego blocks or standard-type blocks.

Setting Priorities

Setting priorities also means looking at your expectations of your child and reexamining and changing your expectations of yourself and your home. Everyone likes to have nice things and a nice home, yet we recognize the necessity of keeping knick-knacks out of the reach of a toddler. Living with a hyperactive child is a lot like living with a toddler. More than 50 percent of all hyperactive children have coordination problems, and they are clumsy and klutzy at times. They can knock over a valuable vase or a fragile glass sculpture before they even know it is there. If you have something of great value, keep it on display in your room or somewhere else that is off-limits to your children.

When a child destroys something of great value, parents can find themselves very upset with the child and themselves. You may get so mad that you yell at the child or spank him without thinking. We've all done it. Many times you will have to force yourself into a proper perspective by asking yourself, *What's more important to me, the vase or my child's self-concept?* In reality we all know that they are both important to us. But it is natural to ask why the child couldn't be just a little more careful around things we value or that are worth so much. As we said before, it is important to keep anything of great personal value in your room or another place off-limits to children, and perhaps you will want to consider the following solution to the problem of destruction of items of monetary value.

Suppose it really upsets you to see your child walk on the new sofa for which you have saved for two years. Understandably, any parent would be angry, but you will be a lot less angry if you buy a nice sofa secondhand. It may not be your dream piece, but try to remember that the more expensive new sofa that is your dream piece and covered not just in your favorite fabric, but also in two years of saving and self-denial, will not look like a "dream piece" for very long with your child walking on it. Yes, you will be able to train your hyperactive child not to walk on furniture, but these children are impulsive and lapses and accidents happen even with the well-trained child. While your hyperactive child is young, buy your furniture at moving sales and garage sales, not expensive antique stores.

The same concept is true for toys and clothing for your hyperactive child. You can expect your hyperactive child to take care of his clothes and his toys, but you will not feel as upset if your child rips the pair of two-dollar overalls you got at a garage sale as you would if he rips the new pair that cost twenty-eight dollars. Buying nice things used will save more than money; it will save your nerves, your family, and your child's self-esteem.

Setting Task Priorities

Sometimes you find yourself setting priorities for all kinds of things: school, home, family, and yourself. For your child you may set priorities like the following:

- Study and do homework.
- Remember to hand in homework.
- Get ready for bed.

- Clean up after himself.
- Get off to school without a hassle.
- Clean the bathroom.
- Turn off lights.
- Put down the toilet seat.

First, eliminate any tasks that are not totally necessary, like "turn off the lights" or "put down the toilet seat," or you may just postpone working on them for the time being. Next you will want to look at your list of tasks to do and list them according to priorities. What are the most important things your child has to do? Homework?

HOMEWORK

If you feel doing homework is the most important, you will want to find the skills your child has mastered already and use them as part of adapting the task breakdown.

- Does Johnny have an appropriate place to work? An organized desk or area with few distractions is best.
- Does he have all of the materials he needs and are they organized properly?
- Does he go to his room and *start* his homework when told?
- Does he need help getting started?
- Does he stay on-task? What happens after he starts his work?

After you have set priorities, you will want to structure your child's environment to help maximize his chance of success.

Structuring or Organizing the Environment

Structuring Your Child's Room

Perhaps the best place to begin organizing your child's environment is where he spends a lot of his time—his room. Cleaning the bedroom is always a problem for hyperactive children. They look at the mess and do not know where to begin, but they can and will do a much better job if you break this job into small parts and make sure that each part is highly organized.

TOY STORAGE

Dividing toys in boxes or bins is a good place to start. Regular cardboard boxes that you can pick up in the grocery store can be covered in contact paper and used as storage bins, or you can buy plastic dishpans or the more expensive storage bins if you wish. These can be used to hold Lego blocks, Tinkertoy blocks, Ramagons, or other multiple-piece toys. A picture on the front of the bin, either drawn or cut out from the original toy box and taped on, will also visually remind the child that Lego blocks belong in that box. Another trick nursery school teachers use is to trace larger one-piece toys, like trucks or one-piece games, on colored construction paper and tape the outline or "shadow" to a shelf with clear contact paper. The child now knows exactly where that toy is supposed to be put away. Labeling the narrow edge of the shelf with the name of the toy to go there is helpful also. All of these techniques are meant to reach the child on many levels and are multisensory in approach.

The *multisensory approach* uses as many of the senses as possible, often pairing senses together: visual with auditory (looking at pie being cut as someone explains fractions), or visual with tactile (seeing and touching, sandpaper letters) or visual, auditory, and tactile (using a talking computer while playing an on-screen game).

Try to keep things interesting and as handy for the child as possible. A child is far more likely to hang up his clothes on a hook that is at his height and attached to a Captain Hook plaque than a regular hook that is placed at adult level.

Be creative; make a "pajama doll" for your child. You can use an old Halloween costume (a one-piece that covers the whole body) and attach a stuffed animal head to it. By stuffing the legs and arms, you can create a place (the body cavity) for your child to "stuff" his pajamas.

Structuring a Place for Homework

Somewhere around third or fourth grade, children start getting homework assignments and parents start to realize the importance of having an organized place for their child to do assignments and study. When the time comes, you will want to structure a place for your child to do his homework. It is always best to plan and set up a homework spot *with* your child. Hyperactive children aren't always comfortable in a straight-backed chair at a desk. Some children are quick to tell you they are most comfortable lying on the floor or sitting in an easy chair to do their homework. Parents have to listen to and respect their child's wishes on this topic.

It is not always a good idea to send the hyperactive child off to his room to do homework. For many children, doing homework in a quiet place where Mom and/or Dad is around "supervising" will prove more productive. Remember, hyperactive children have difficulty staying on-task, and they also work best in one-on-one situations. Perhaps doing homework at the dining room table or some other area that is not busy but can be seen by Mom and/or Dad is a good idea. The parent's visual presence is a reminder to stay on-task, and frequent words of encouragement are helpful.

Whether you and your child design a study area in the corner of the room with a beanbag chair or at a desk with a straight-backed chair in the child's room, you will want to make a place with the needed materials close by. Pens, pencils, paper, and other materials need to be within reach in an organized setup.

Inexpensive little plastic baskets are excellent organizers for homework materials. They can be stacked or placed on nearby shelves for handy access.

Organizing the Notebook

While getting homework done is certainly a major part of the battle to obtain success in school, there are two other components playing a major role: making sure the child knows what to do (writing down correct assignments) and handing in assignments. You will have a lot more success with homework if parent and child pay some careful attention to organizing the "notebook."

Many schools will provide assignment notebooks for the child—weekly sheets look like a large five-day calendar with blank blocks for each subject (seven boxes down and five across). Parents can make them for next to nothing using a plain piece of paper. For ADHD children it is easier for them to keep track of something that stays in their three-ring binder in a specific place rather than a small separate book that they must take out, write the assignment in, and put away again. We will say it many times in this book and more thoroughly in later chapters, but ADHD children are more successful when steps and complications are kept to a minimum.

Pouches are a handy item to keep in the three-ring binder. Students can keep pencils, pens, erasers, and other easily lost little items in these vinyl or cloth zip bags.

ASSIGNMENTS—THEIR PLACE IN THE NOTEBOOK

On a good day, Max wrote down his assignments, followed his study schedule, completed his homework, and still came home from school with a note from the teacher saying he was missing three assignments and was currently getting a C or D because of it. Not only did the Kennedys know Max had done his assignments; they had checked them, so they knew he had done his best and had high-effort work to hand in.

"Max, what happened?" his parents asked. "We know you did these assignments. What happened here?"

After the initial rounds of "I don't know," Max's parents went back to square one and asked more specific questions in search of more specific answers: "Where did you put your paper when you finished it? . . . Okay, you put it in your math book. Did the book make it to school? Did you take it out of the book and hand it to the teacher? . . . All right, this teacher has you put it in a basket. Did you put it in the right basket?"

Just as they had to ask specific questions to locate Max's completed homework assignments, they soon discovered that Max was losing his assignments in his books or in his notebook. Max needed a specific place to put his work. The solution was pockets.

Pockets are dividerlike sections that go into a three-ring binder and have a pocket on either side of the heavy manila paper. Using them like subject dividers, you will want a pocket for each subject. Utilizing these pockets, the Kennedys labeled one side "Work to Be Done" and the other side of the pocket "Work to Be Handed In." For Max this was an enormous help. These pockets provided specific places for Max to put his completed work. He no longer had to fish through his textbook or notebook looking for a piece of paper, which to him probably looked like every other piece of paper, to find his assignments.

But how do you get *your* child interested in pockets? Children are most willing to work with ideas they come up with themselves. So you could try asking your child if he has any ideas on how he could remember to hand in his homework. Let's look at the following example:

Max, what do you think you could do to remember to hand in your homework?

Maybe I should put it in the front of my math book.

Well, it is a good idea to always keep it in the same spot every day. That way you know exactly where it is, but sometimes you leave your math book in your locker, and papers fall out of textbooks easily. Is there another book that you could put it in?

I could put it in my notebook, but it might fall out of that, too.

I know something we could put the homework in that would keep it from falling out. They're pocketlike dividers. We can use your idea with that.

All of us learn and remember things we discover on our own, or through our own experience. While hyperactive children need to be very actively involved in learning, they may have difficulty coming up with ideas on how to organize their notebooks (or their rooms), so be prepared with ideas of your own as well.

NOTEBOOK REVIEW

It is a good idea to go through your child's notebook with him once a week. Use the notebook review night to decide with your child which papers should be discarded and which ones kept. Weekly "pruning" of the notebook will provide more than an opportunity to keep the notebook cleaned out. It is also an opportunity to go through papers with your child and see how he is doing on classroom assignments. This is especially important in junior high and high school, when communication with teachers is likely to be less frequent and problems can go unnoticed.

On one of the Kennedy family's weekend reviews they found a note from one of Max's teachers: "Max, this is well written and the thoughts are well organized, but your handwriting is so bad I can't give you any higher than a B." If Max had told his teacher of his motor disability or if he had typed his report, his grade would have been much higher. After his parents knew there was a problem, they encouraged Max to do all of his assignments for that class on the computer, raising his grade to the A he had worked hard for.

Lockers

Lockers can be a black hole in an ADHD child's life. "Things" seem to disappear in a locker and are never seen again. There are ways to organize even the messiest locker. Parents can purchase adjustable locker shelves. These shelves are inexpensive and almost indispensable if your child has to share a locker. Usually, variety stores like Walmart or K Mart have them. You can label the thin edge of the shelf with the course name of books to be stored there: math, language, science, et cetera. Once your child is in the habit of always putting his math book on the same shelf, it is not as likely to be tossed into the "black hole" of the locker.

Older children may find it embarrassing to have "labels" on their locker shelves. Talk to your child. Would he rather have a code system or special book covers with matching pictures? You can work out a code with your child: *M* for math book, *S* for science, et cetera. You may even want to write the letter on the shelf edge with a felt-tip pen in graffiti style or have a color code. You can buy self-sticking dots in the paper and notebook department. By placing a green dot on the shelf and a green dot on the science book, your child will know the science book goes on the shelf with the green dot.

Lockers are also a good place to keep bundles of extra pens and pencils so they will be available when they have "magically disappeared" from the notebook pouch. If you store extra pencils and pens in the locker be sure to keep them organized and accessible. It does no good to have them if they can't be found easily.

Lost and Found

Hyperactive children are always losing things: homework assignments, pens, lunches, and jackets. We've already discussed some ideas on how to keep track of homework assignments and the materials children need for classwork. While losing pens, pencils, and lunches can be truly annoying, it is just that, an annoyance, but losing a jacket means an expense. At today's prices, no one can afford to replace a child's jacket every time the weather turns warm and he takes it off and leaves it somewhere.

One way to make jackets more identifiable is to have the child's last name printed across the back, like the football players do. For nothing more than the cost of the letters any T-shirt shop will do this for you, even if you've purchased the jacket elsewhere. At a total cost of three to five dollars, it's a bargain compared to replacing a fifty- or sixty-dollar jacket.

Always make your child part of the process. Take him to the T-shirt store to pick out the style and color of letters. Most children, especially children who have played team sports, are perfectly happy to have their last name printed "player style" across the back of their jacket. Jackets with someone's last name on them usually appear in the lost and found very quickly.

Organizing Time

Parents of hyperactive children often complain that their children waste enormous amounts of time daydreaming. Part of that problem is that they grow tired of what they are doing very rapidly, but another part is that they do not organize their time well. It is very important for ADHD children to have a sense of what comes next, that every day they follow the same pattern:

> Every morning Mom wakes me up. I go downstairs, eat my breakfast, brush my teeth, and go back upstairs and put on the clothes I picked out last night. Then I pick up my backpack that I packed my books and homework in last night and walk to the corner to catch the bus.

Here again, organizing your child's time is something you must do with your child. It is his time, and for this to work well, he will need an active voice in how it is spent. For an easily distracted ADHD child, ten minutes is difficult to judge. Many times the rest of the family is on a tight schedule, too, and the twenty minutes it takes the ADHD child to eat a ten-minute breakfast can put everyone into a tailspin. A small wind-up timer, like you use for baking, can be helpful to give the hyperactive child a better sense of time. Timers where a child can hear the ticking and see the dial move toward the 0, then hear a bell make the abstract concept of "ten minutes to eat" more visibly tangible.

You will want to look at all of the things your child has to do in a given day: homework, chores, projects, fun time, dinner- and family time, homework, and evening activities. Extra activities like scouts, religious education, lessons, school programs, or sport activities may change from day to day or week to week, but you will need to allow for them in the schedule. You will want to go through what has to be done and give your child a voice in when it is done.

All children have to do homework, but your child may need to do something else for a while when he first gets home. The Kennedys have one child who did homework immediately after she got home. Their hyperactive child, Max, needed to watch TV first or go out to work on his treehouse; then he did homework in thirty-minute chunks. Your child may be unable to just sit down and do his homework all at once. Many hyperactive children may need to do mental work in fifteen-minute "chunks" and go do physical work like chores or projects in between chunks of homework. This is fine: after all, he is getting it done. Alternating mental and physical activities in fifteen-minute "chunks" allows many hyperactive children to be more productive. Different children have different styles, and as long as they are getting their work done, they should be rewarded.

ADHD children do best when they have a schedule, and often they will want to follow that schedule even when it has to change. Be sure to discuss any necessary changes in a schedule ahead of time with the child to ease his adjustment as much as possible. Habits, both good and bad, are formed fairly easily with ADHD children. It is important to form good habits with them (homework every day, bath every other night, et cetera) by rewarding them.

While most hyperactive children do like to be busy, make sure they do not get overwhelmed with too much activity. Creating a balance that keeps the child stimulated and active is important, but always keep in mind that you do not want to get your child wound up; so, once again, prioritize. As mentioned before, setting priorities is important for him and for you as a parent. It is very important for you to know which activities are important to him. If your child likes karate lessons, soccer, or scouts, make sure that activity has a place in the schedule. Providing a successful and enjoyable experience will go a long way toward building his self-esteem and social adjustment.

Using token reward systems to reward the fun activities as well as the chores is important also. Tokens enable everyone to "see" how well this child is doing in a given task, which bring us to our next means of making life a little easier and a lot more fulfilling for our ADHD child.

Feedback in the Form of Praise and Rewards

A positive self-concept, or how the child sees himself, is one of the major keys to helping the hyperactive child improve his behavior and his chance for success in life. While we have always known that a positive self-concept plays a role in the success children find as adults, we know that it plays an especially important role for hyperactive children. Praising the child for any job well done, or even done sufficiently, has to become part of a parent's daily routine. To build a positive self-concept, parents have to be quicker with praise than they are with criticism. Praise and rewards has to be the first course of action for parents, but rewards can be tricky.

Parents need to know what the child sees as a reward. It can be different from what the parent sees as a reward. If you say to Johnny, "If you skip school one more time, they will expel you," Johnny will feel he is being rewarded with exactly what he wants: he gets out of school. You see being expelled as a punishment, but Johnny sees it as a reward.

In a different vein, rewards should *remain* rewards and not turn into nonrewarding situations for the child. One mother chose to reward her son with a visit to the home of his friend who had moved away. This would have been a wonderful activity-oriented reward, except it required a six-hour car ride, which quickly became very unpleasant. It would have been far better to reward him with a visit from his friend.

Give a reward immediately, even if it is just a token reward. Hyperactive children have difficulty delaying gratification. When a parent promises them a Nintendo game if they go to bed on time every day for a month, the parent is asking the impossible. No matter how great the reward, if it is not immediate, it is lost. A token system that gives the child an immediate reward, one he can touch and hold or look at and count, is necessary. You can still promise him a Nintendo, but it is far better to say that when he has collected thirty marbles, one of which you will give him each night he goes to bed on time, he can cash them in for a Nintendo game. A month is a very long time when you are a child who deals with *now, this minute,* better than any other time frame.

Token rewards and consequences are of vital importance to the hyperactive child both at home and in school. At home you will want to reward your child for doing his homework, for getting good grades, for doing his chores, and for working with his brothers and sisters. Recent research indicates that hyperactive children grow tired of the same reward and after a while they will not work for the same reward anymore. You will have better success if you rotate the token you are using for rewards and consequences. You may want to give your child stickers one week, pennies the next week, dinosaur sponges another week, pieces of a puzzle the fourth week, Lego pieces the fifth week, etc. Having about eight to ten different sets of tokens is a good idea. Using tokens means giving rewards for effort and success and taking tokens away when necessary. An added advantage of multipiece tokens like a Lego set or a puzzle is that the pieces can be given out one at a time and they can be used as a group reward in the family or at school. Other family members or class members can also receive pieces for rewards. Multipiece tokens can be returned when a consequence is necessary. Behavioral charts are great because they serve as visual reminders as well as tokens. When the child is earning pennies, Lego blocks, or something else, you may wish to keep an ongoing chart and use checks or pluses in spaces as a visual reminder for the child of how many pennies he has earned or how many Lego pieces he has accumulated.

Supervision

Now that you have broken down tasks, set priorities, structured the environment, organized your child's time, paired stimuli, and provided feedback, you may well wonder if you will ever reach the point where you can just send your child to his room to do his homework and expect him to come out with it all done, put it in his backpack, and remember to take it to school with him the next morning. What you are longing for is behavior like that of a normal child. What you have to remember is: Yes, this child will improve with structure. Yes, someday he will be able to function independently, with some help getting started and a little more supervision in his work than most "normal" people. You will still have to monitor him, even in the most organized of environments. But by following the suggestions in this chapter, you will provide means for him to function much better, and he will learn eventually that with practice and help he can do some of the organizing himself.

| CHAPTER **6** | *Discipline: There Is a Difference* |

Discipline is one of the biggest problems facing the parents of hyperactive children, probably because the hyperactive child requires so much of it. Parents are quick to tell you stories like this:

> With my other children, I could tell them one time, "Don't do that," and they would stop. But Johnny, my hyperactive child, I could tell him a hundred times, "Johnny, don't carve soap with my potato peeler," "Don't paint the house with used motor oil," or, "Don't walk on Grandma's white sofa in your muddy shoes," but he still does it. It's like every day is a brand-new day and yesterday's rules are long forgotten. The next time he feels like painting the house he might not use motor oil (he probably used it all before), but he will use the first can of whatever he finds, whether it is white paint or molasses. I just cannot stay one step ahead of him. He does things my other kids never thought of.

One of the major characteristics of hyperactive children, impulsivity, is at the root of many of the behavioral problems with which parents must cope. It is another problem, the apparent inability to learn from past mistakes, that frustrates parents the most. As this wearied mother stated, every day is a brand-new day, and the consequences of behavior are long since forgotten.

As parents of hyperactive children, we all wonder if these children will ever figure out "cause and effect." If they do, will they ever be able to control their impulsive behavior long enough to allow the knowledge of the "effect" to change their course of action?

Hyperactive children create the same discipline problems in school as at home. One kindergarten teacher, renowned for her patience and understanding, tearfully confessed to a mother, "In twenty-one years of teaching I have never spanked a child, except Max." Max was hyperactive. She wondered out loud to Max's mother as she apologized, "Could Mother Theresa spend a day with him without spanking him?"

Anyone living with a hyperactive child has probably spanked that child at least once; none of us are saints. While there is no question that a hyperactive child would stretch the patience of a saint, there are better solutions than spanking. There has to be, because with most hyperactive children, spanking does not work. Even if it did work when the child was small, it would not work for long. Eventually the child will become too big to spank. If he has learned that the way "big people" handle frustration is to physically strike out, can we expect him to behave differently? All too often we spank because we are angered by the child's behavior. He has driven us past the limit of our tolerance and we are so upset that we can no longer think, so we react. When we spank, we are modeling the very behavior that causes our hyperactive children so much difficulty: impulsivity. Hyperactive children are different, and so are their disciplinary needs. If we want to improve their behavior, we need to rethink the way we discipline them.

Parents have to change from a verbal and reaction-oriented form of discipline to a positive, intervening action form of discipline. That means not waiting until something has happened and you have to react to it, but stepping in before something happens and doing something or saying something that will change what will happen.

When Words Are Not Enough

Most of us try to parent and discipline the way we were taught
or educated to believe is the best way: by sitting down with the
child and verbally explaining. In the case of a five-year-old hyperactive little girl, most of us would handle this situation in
the following manner:

> Suzie, you need to be nice to Jenny when she comes to
> play with you. She doesn't like it when you grab her Play-
> Doh. She wants you to share and talk to her about what
> you want instead of grabbing. Okay?

Here again, it was the impulsive behavior that caused the problem for the hyperactive child. Suzie saw the Play-Doh; she
wanted it; so she grabbed it. As good parents, we responded
verbally with an explanation. But all of us who have hyperactive
children know that talking alone does not work. Most of us will
try to continue the "good parent" method, and we'll tell Suzie
three or four times, "Suzie, don't grab Jenny's Play-Doh." Each
time our explanation gets shorter, as does our patience. By the
fourth or fifth time, we're ready to swat Suzie's bottom and
send Jenny home. Suzie's in tears, Jenny's in tears, and Mom's
close to tears.

We already know that Suzie's problem is impulsive behavior,
but Mom has a problem, too: she is responding verbally to a
child that needs more than verbal input. By the time Mom's
reached her limit she may believe that what Suzie needs is a
good spanking, but what Suzie really needs is adult intervention
at crucial times in her play with Jenny. How do we do that?
We do that by applying some of the rules of discipline.

With our other, "normal" children, we practice patience, but
with a hyperactive child that very "patience" can cause us to
wait just a little too long, while a situation deteriorates in seconds
as we watch. You have to develop a sixth sense that tells you
when to step in, and it is usually at the first sign of trouble.

When Suzie grabbed Jenny's Play-Doh the first time, Mom needed to stop what she was doing and go over and sit with Suzie and Jenny for a few minutes. If more Play-Doh was available, Mom should have said, "Suzie, if you need more, we'll get some from the box. You don't need to take Jenny's. Jenny needs her Play-Doh to make and build her ideas." If there was not any extra, Mom could convince Suzie she had all she needed: "You don't need much to make a snail," or, "We can take just a tiny bit and use the little cookie cutter." Notice Mom has not commented on Suzie's bad behavior yet; instead, she has offered positive input, telling Suzie what she can do.

Mom needs to stick around just a little longer, and when the play is going smoothly again she needs to make sure Suzie knows it: "Suzie, you and Jenny are playing so nicely together. I really like that. And because you play so well, I am going to give you a gold star on your chart." Giving an immediate reward for good behavior should always be the first course of action.

With hyperactive children, it is almost always necessary to pair verbal praise with a more tangible reward: a gold star, a sticker, or something else the child can see or hold. A reward is part of good discipline because it helps to eliminate the need for discipline while building a positive self-image in the child.

Of course we both know that our hyperactive Suzie is going to grab Jenny's Play-Doh as soon as Mom leaves. Suzie has already made ten little cookies out of her Play-Doh, and Jenny still has some, so once again Suzie will grab and leave Jenny with nothing but a scream. What should Mom do now? Again, action must be coupled with the verbal response, which must be a criticism of the behavior, not the child. We used rewards first. Now Suzie needs to face a consequence, in this case a time-out. Mom needs to remove Suzie from the dough activity while explaining to Suzie, "Suzie, I am sorry, but you can't take Jenny's Play-Doh because you ran out. You seem to be having some trouble sharing the Play-Doh, so you'll have to stop playing with it for a while. You'll have to sit in the chair for five minutes." Mom needs to put Suzie in a chair with a timer set on five minutes where Suzie can watch the minutes go by.

Most psychology books stop right here, because average children are willing to stop here. Normal children would learn from the five minutes' time-out, sit quietly in the chair, then return to play. Hyperactive children are different.

Parents of hyperactive children see the differences every day in the way their children respond to situations. Anyone who has a hyperactive child would look at what is happening with Suzie and say two things: "My child would take the timer apart," and, "What makes you think she will stay in that chair?" Some hyperactive children would take the timer apart, and Suzie may be one of them, so put the timer where she can see it but not touch it. All hyperactive children would get out of the chair, so how do you keep her in the chair without spanking her when she gets out? You tell her you will add a minute every time she gets out of the chair. You may have to physically put her back in the chair a couple of times, but eventually she will make the "cause and effect" connection. Mom has to make sure she adds the minute each time Suzie gets out of the chair, too. It is very important to do what you say you are going to do. Be consistent. In the example involving Suzie and Jenny, we used a number of basic disciplinary principles to change Suzie's behavior.

- Mom told Suzie what she could do.
- Mom used an immediate and *incidental* reward to reinforce the good behavior.
- Mom criticized only the behavior, not the child, which helps Suzie maintain a positive self-concept.
- Mom had a consequence for continuing undesirable behavior (no Play-Doh and a time-out in a chair).

Also, Mom used some extra techniques that are necessary with hyperactive children. She paired verbal praise (reward) with a tangible, visual reward (the gold star). Hyperactive children must be taught through as many of the senses as possible. A lot of hyperactive children have been through years of ear infections. For them, the auditory/verbal mode of learning is not enough, and discipline is, after all, learned behavior.[1] Almost all hyperactive children are very tactile. They love to touch, to feel whatever they are involved in. In almost all cases, it is necessary to use more than verbal/auditory input (talking and explaining) to reach the hyperactive child with the message. If possible include something tactile, something he can touch— marbles, stickers, pennies, stars, anything you like. This does not mean you should abandon explanations or verbal discussion with the child, but remember, keep it short and pair the verbal with something else.

Basic Techniques of Discipline

Knowing some of the basic techniques of discipline and understanding why we use them can be very helpful to parents. We mentioned a few as we looked at a better way to handle Suzie's aggressive behavior. These techniques cannot cure hyperactivity, but they will help make your child easier to live with and make your days with your child more pleasant. Living with a hyperactive child is not easy. There will be days when you have used all of these techniques and you have still had a horrible day with Johnny. Do not give up. These techniques work, and the number of good days will start to increase while the number of horrible days will shrink.

Use a System of Rewards and Consequences

Some normal children do not require consequences, and for them a reward system alone will keep them on the straight and narrow. Many hyperactive children do not respond to rewards alone. They seem to need a consequence to nudge their motivational energy along. A consequence should be a logical result of behavior, not necessarily a natural one. If your child sticks his chewed gum in the piano, he does not get gum for a month. If he breaks his sister's toy, he buys her a new one. If he watched

TV instead of doing his homework, he does not see TV for a day. There is a difference between a logical consequence and a natural consequence. The natural consequence of not doing your homework is failing the course. Adult perspective tells us that failing the course is a very harsh and complex consequence for a child who is already unhappy with school. Parents need to use their judgment and find logical consequences that are more meaningful to the child, such as loss of privileges. As parents, we need to separate rights from privileges. Children have a right to love, food, shelter, and clothing. Toys, TVs, phones, and car keys are all privileges and can be taken away as a means of age-appropriate discipline. Always inform the child of the consequence before you enact it: "If you stay home from school because you think you're sick, you stay in bed, and you do not see TV." Be sure to follow through on consequences. If you have to leave the child home alone because you are at work, unplug the cable so he cannot watch TV.

When it is age-appropriate (usually five to eleven years of age), have your child take a part in deciding what would be the best consequence for his behavior. Sometimes role reversal is a good way to do this: "Billy, if you were the mom and your son shaved your expensive decorative candle, then melted the shavings over the stove and left melted wax everywhere, ruined your pan, and poured the hot wax into his sister's Play-Doh molds and melted them, what would you do?"

Usually, the child will suggest a consequence far more severe than his parent's.

If I were the mom, I guess I would like the candle the way it was, huh?

Oh, yes. It was a special Christmas candle.

I think I wouldn't give that little boy any Christmas presents, and I would make him tell his mom and his sister he was sorry.

Well, I am sure his mom still loves him and he will get some Christmas presents, but don't you think he should buy his sister some new Play-Doh molds? Maybe he should clean the stove off, too, and clean the pan he used to melt the wax, as well as telling his mom and sister he's sorry.

Part of Billy's extreme consequence is a trial balloon he is sending up to see if he still has a home and if someone at home is still going to give him Christmas presents. Another part of the consequence Billy suggested was an honest recognition that he had done something for which he was sorry. If the child is at an appropriate age, it can be very helpful to let him take part in deciding the consequences of his behavior, especially for the following reason. Hyperactive children often have difficulty understanding how other people see them or their actions. Role reversal allows your child to pretend he is you and that you are him. This technique can go a long way toward helping the child understand how you feel about an incident and why you feel that way.

When Billy's mother suggested that Billy clean up the stove and all the wax, she was using another very important technique. She *allowed the child to take responsibility* for his actions. This technique accomplishes two very important goals: It teaches the child responsibility and allows him to make amends for his actions, and it relieves the parents of some of the anger and hostility we feel when we spend the day cleaning up after the wake of a hurricane. It is much easier to remain calm if you know he has to clean up the milk he spilled or scrub the wall he wrote on.

Keep Things Positive

Suzie's mom was very careful to word things as positively as possible: "You are having trouble sharing; you need to share; you cannot take Jenny's Play-Doh." She criticized what Suzie was doing, but not Suzie. Mom never said, "Suzie, you are a bad girl. Do not do that." If a child thinks she is bad, she will do bad things, but if she thinks she is good but does bad things from time to time, she is more likely to try to reconcile her behavior with her positive self-concept. Mom told Suzie exactly what she could and could not do, but in a positive way that gave Suzie more direction. She worded it in the positive. It is always better to give a positive direction than a negative order: "Get off the couch, and put your feet on the floor," instead of, "Do not walk on my couch." In the first example a child is given an action to follow, not one to stop. Parents of hyperactive children feel as though they are constantly saying "stop" and "don't." You will feel better and so will the child if you word things in the positive. Suzie will see herself as a good kid who took her friend's Play-Doh. Mom leaves Suzie's self-concept intact. Billy's mom also kept things positive. She reassured Billy by telling him she still loved him. She suggested some positive steps he could take, and she encouraged him to look at the situation more positively.

Outside the home hyperactive children find themselves in situations and with playmates that tear down their self-concept. As parents we have little or no control over these mentally battering situations; however, we can control how we discipline our children. It is important to keep that discipline as positive as possible.

Always Reward Good Behavior Immediately

This is another very important point. Parents of hyperactive children sometimes have a hard time finding their child doing anything good, but one of the ways we build self-confidence and a positive self-image in our children is by telling them when they have done something right. Parents can grow so used to watching a hyperactive child closely to head off all of his bad performances that they forget to focus in on the good things he does. Most children do manage to do something good once in a while. We need to watch for those good deeds, no matter how few and far between they are. Praise your hyperactive child, even if it is just for taking out the garbage: "Thank you for taking out the garbage, Jane. You were a good helper, and I appreciate it."

Use Activity-Oriented Rewards

All children have things they really like to do: play miniature golf or go to a park across town, the zoo, or a special movie. Rewards that involve physical activity or time spent with the family or special time spent alone with one parent offer parents almost as much of a reward as the child. Physical activities like golf, swimming and baseball are activities you can do with your child. If your child likes the activity and is even minimally good at it, the activity will offer many chances for praise. While at the park, parents can comment on what a good climber Jimmy is or how strong his legs must be to be able to swing so high. At the very least, physical activities will use some of that unspent energy and make the child feel good about himself.

Family-oriented activities offer another kind of reward to the child and family. Imagine how good it makes a hyperactive child feel to hear Mom or Dad say; "We're going to the movies tonight because Tom made it to the bus on time every day this week." Tom's prestige goes up a notch or two in the eyes of his siblings if his brothers and sisters get a special treat because of something Tom did.

Time spent alone with one parent can be a special reward, too, especially if both parents work or there are a lot of children in the family. Try to find a special activity to center the "one-on-one" activity around, like a bicycle ride and picnic or a cave-hunting hike with Mom or Dad.

Never Give Food as an Immediate Reward

More than twenty years ago psychologists recognized the danger of using food as a reward. Children who are given food as an immediate reward will "reward" themselves with food as adults; for many this will result in eating disorders. That does not mean you cannot take your child out for dinner on his birthday or allow him to have a special dish or dessert on holidays. What it does mean is that you should not give your child an M&M's candy every time he brings home an A or a candy bar every time he has behaved in the supermarket. Immediate rewards are quickly associated with activities and the good feelings that go with the situation, so make sure the immediate reward is not food.

Draw Up a Discipline Plan Ahead of Time

Sit down with your spouse, baby-sitter, and anyone else who spends a large part of the day with your child and draw up a disciplinary plan. Think about what behaviors you want to eliminate and which behaviors you want to encourage. If you want to encourage your child to be kind to his brother, reward him every time he does the least little thing that is nice. If he gives his brother his leftover cake, reward him; if he says something kind to his brother, make sure he knows you noticed it. Decide which behaviors require a consequence, and decide what those consequences will be. Different personalities will approach parenting differently; that is okay, just as long as the rules, range of rewards, and consequences remain consistent.

Part of being consistent is making sure your child is not getting mixed messages. Discipline can be successful only if both parents agree on consequences and rewards and when both will be given. If Dad sticks to the plan and Mom does not back him up, Dad will look like the bad guy. That is not fair to Dad. Children learn very quickly who is the "tough guy" in the family, and they will hit on the softy every time. Even the best disciplinary plan can be destroyed by a child who has already learned the divide-and-conquer maneuver. Hyperactive children are masters at the fine art of manipulation. When they have learned to combine their incredible persistence with their manipulative skills, they can destroy almost any parent's resolve. Therefore, it becomes crucially important that parents stick together and support each other in discipline.

When Mom and Dad do not agree on a consequence or even

a reward, it is important for them to discuss it privately, and ahead of time. If Tom keeps missing the school bus because he lollygags on the way to the bus stop, Mom and Dad should plan a reward and a consequence on Friday night, not Monday morning as they watch the school bus leave the neighborhood without Tom. They will need to plan a token reward for every day that Tom makes it to the bus on time and an activity for which Tom can exchange his stars or stickers (token). Also, they need to plan a logical consequence in the unhappy event that Tom misses the bus every day for a week. Make sure the consequence is not something Tom may consider a reward (missing school) or one that causes more harm than good (not letting him go to the only birthday party he has been invited to in three years). Have him walk to school, if that is at all practical, or do a chore like clean out the car for Mom.

Avoid Open-ended Decisions

Part of growing up is learning to make decisions. All children, including hyperactive children, learn to make decisions by making them, good and bad. But the poorly thought out or impulsive decisions of hyperactive children usually result in arguments and ultimately require disciplinary action. However, this might be avoided if the parent avoids open-ended decisions that leave the child free to make his own, potentially disastrous, decisions. As an example, let's look at what happens with six-year-old Molly on a special school day:

Molly, hurry up and finish your breakfast. You have to get ready for school, and remember today is the day your class is going on a field trip to the dairy farm.

Can I wear a dress, Mom?

I don't think a dress is a very good idea. It is still pretty cold outside, and a farm is pretty messy.

For an average child, Mom's warning would have been all that was necessary, but for a hyperactive child, the lack of direction and limitation in Mom's warning will result in trouble.

Molly, what are you doing in that sundress?

I want to wear my pretty dress to the farm.

Molly, it's still February, for pete's sake. You'll freeze to death. Take it off right now and put on something warm. Hurry up. The bus will be here any minute.

I want to wear the dress. You said I could.

I did not. I said you couldn't. I told you it was too cold. Now, take it off and get some slacks on. You are going to be late.

This "misunderstanding" will result in many things: There will be a big argument; Molly will have a temper tantrum complete with kicking, crying, and screaming; and Mom will have to drive her to school because she is so late. While Molly may end up wearing the slacks, she and Mom both will have a rotten day because of all the early morning turmoil. Mom's two other children were not hyperactive, and she thinks it is not good to tell children "no," so she uses subtle nuances and gives solid reasons. When Mom said, "That's not a good idea," she thought she was saying, "Do not wear a dress," in a positive way. Molly thought she was telling her what "her idea" was. Molly's idea was a dress, and if Mom's idea is different, that will not stop Molly. Mom's approach would have been wonderful for her two other children, but it did not work with Molly for a reason. Hyperactive children do not pick up nuances. They need precise direction and positive limitations. In other words, they need parents to decide what decisions they will get to make and what choices are offered. What would have been a better way to handle the problem? The night before, Mom should have gone into Molly's room.

Molly, tomorrow is your field trip to the dairy farm. Let's pick out your clothes now. It is still pretty cold, so you'll need to wear slacks and a long-sleeved top. Do you want to wear your blue slacks or your green ones, or how about your yellow cords with the chickens on them?

I want to wear my sundress. It's pretty.

You know the rules, Molly. Long sleeves and slacks if the temperature is below seventy degrees. Warm clothes in the winter, cool clothes, like sundresses, in the summer when it is over seventy degrees. Now, what do you want to wear?

I want to wear my sundress.

That is not one of the choices. It can be one of the choices when it is over seventy degrees, but not now.

Can I wear the blue top with the yellow chicken pants?

Sure, that is a good choice. We'll put a yellow ribbon on the collar. Pick out some socks and panties, too, so you'll be all ready for tomorrow.

This time Mom applied some of those basic techniques of discipline and avoided the need for discipline altogether. She let Molly make her own decision, but she limited the options Molly had to choose from ones that were acceptable. She organized beforehand. You can avoid a lot of problems if you organize as much as possible ahead of time. She reminded Molly of the rules, some very specific rules (long sleeves and slacks if the temperature is below seventy degrees). Everything was very clear; nothing was left to Molly's interpretation, not even the definition of warm clothes (long sleeves and slacks). Molly could very well feel that the sundress would have been warm enough. Mom kept things positive. When Molly still wanted to wear the sundress, Mom reminded her that a sundress was not one of the choices, but it would be when the temperature was over seventy degrees. Again, Mom was specific. She gave Molly a positive stroke, telling her she made a good choice. Mom did another thing: She chose her battle. She did not fight over the top, even though she knew it would not match. She knew that the only thing worth fighting over was the sundress. Mom helped Molly develop decision-making skills, but by narrowing the choices, she gave Molly a positive experience and made her own day much easier.

Be Consistent

Fear is what children feel when you spank or hit them for their actions, but trust and certainty are what they feel when they know you will do exactly what you say you are going to do. You will have to follow through on promised rewards and consequences. Consistent rules are established before you have to use them, and they are predictable. If you tell a child, "Johnny, if you take apart one more alarm clock, you're going to have to pay for it," you had better be prepared to take Johnny to the bank and have him turn over ten dollars from his savings account. If you tell Johnny, "When you've got ten gold stars on your chart, you can cash them in, and we will take you to the movies," you had better set aside time and money to take Johnny to the movies when he earns that tenth star. Consistent rules remain the same, no matter who is at home watching Johnny. Johnny should know that if he takes apart the alarm clock, someone is going to collect ten dollars, whether it be Mom, Dad, or Carol, the baby-sitter. Being consistent does not mean that you cannot have different parenting styles; you can, but the rules, the occurrence of rewards, and the consequences should be the same.

Age-Appropriate Discipline

There is one last principle of discipline. *Always use age-appropriate discipline.* The methods that work well on a two-year-old do not necessarily work with a fourth-grader, and what works with a fourth-grader will not work with a high school freshman.

Two-to-four-year-olds

Normal two-year-olds are busy, active little creatures, and every parent who has one is convinced their child is hyperactive. It is usually some time after the terrible twos that parents should really begin to suspect hyperactivity. The temper tantrums do not stop, and the social skills do not seem to develop the way they should. Hyperactive children are not interested in "pleasing" their parents and using the potty the way other two-to-three-year-olds do. Somewhere between the ages of two and three, parents of hyperactive children begin to suspect that their child is different. By the time he is four, they know: he is hyperactive.

So, what are the best ways to discipline a hyperactive two-to-four-year-old? Again, some of the basic principles apply.

- Keep things positive.
- Step into the situation before it gets out of hand.
- Reward good behavior *immediately.*
- Give specific, positively worded directions. For example, "keep your feet on the floor," "only color on paper," "tricycles stay outside," or "my pots and pans stay in the kitchen."

There is one other technique that works well with the two-to-three-year-old:

- Ignore bad behavior when you can.

The last one is hard, but it is one of the best ways to eliminate temper tantrums. When your two- or three-year-old goes into a temper tantrum, tell him, "It is okay to kick and scream, but I don't want to see it. So you will have to do this in your bedroom on the floor where it is safe." You will probably have to physically pick him up and carry him to his room, kicking all the way, but as soon as there is no more audience, he will stop. As soon as you eliminate the audience, you have eliminated the reason for a temper tantrum. This works very well at home, but we all know that it will not take long for the child to figure out that temper tantrums work best in the supermarket or in a department store. What can you do then? Your first option is to try to avoid the situation. If your child is prone to temper tantrums, try to avoid long outings in department stores. You cannot avoid the supermarket, so take along something for him to do or play with while he is in the cart. Keep it as a "special" toy, one that he only gets to play with while he is shopping: See and Say and books with tapes work well. Keep your shopping trips short and try to shop when he is well rested and less likely to have a temper tantrum.

When he does have a temper tantrum, stop and think before you act. Ask yourself, *Why is he doing this? What does he want?* Never ignore bad behavior that is destructive to someone else's property or harmful to anyone. However, if he is having a tantrum because he grabbed a box of cookies that he wants, but you do not, whatever you do, do not buy the cookies. Never reward a temper tantrum. If you have to, leave the cart, frozen food and all. Once Pat Kennedy removed her temper-tantrum-stricken son from a cart while calling to the checker on her way out, "I left my cart on aisle two. Please put the ice cream and the meats away. I will be back in an hour or two." She strapped his stiff little body into the car seat and took him home to his room, where he could have his temper tantrum in private. This only happened twice because of the way she handled it.

It is important to reward your child every time you take him shopping and he does not have a temper tantrum: Read him a story when you get home, get out his tricycle, or take him for a bike ride. Be sure and tell him why he is being rewarded: "Jason, you were such a good shopper today, we are going to do something special." Again, make sure it is something the child really likes to do; it needs to be his idea of a reward, not yours.

Parents should not ignore bad behavior in older children. For the most part, it is a bad idea to ignore bad behavior in hyperactive children, but in the case of the two-to-three-year-old with a temper tantrum ignoring temper tantrums is an excellent way to eliminate them.

Five-to-eleven-year-olds

For most parents of hyperactive children, these are probably the most difficult years. These are also the years when the child begins school and, as parents, we begin our interaction with the school. If you are lucky, you have an older child who went through the school first and the school is aware that you are a normal, sane parent with at least one normal child at home. Many parents are not so lucky: If the hyperactive child is the oldest child, the parents must wait until their younger children go through the system before redeeming their good name with teachers and the school system.

There are ways to survive. It is very important to your disciplinary plan to stay in close contact with the school. In the very beginning of every school year, go talk to the teacher immediately. Tell her what your disciplinary plan is. The Kennedys worked out a system with some of their son's teachers that involved tokens given at school. If Max had a good day, the teacher would pin a happy face on his shirt. If Max had a bad day, he got a sad face to bring home. The Kennedys, in turn, gave Max a star on his chart for each happy face he got. When he had ten, twenty, or thirty stars, he could cash them in for Lego blocks of varying costs.

While they did not give allowances, the Kennedys did give the children stickers for jobs and behaviors they wanted them to work on. Max's sister got stickers, too. You may find it necessary to extend the system to all of your children. Even children who are not hyperactive have things to work on. If your daughter would like to stop biting her fingernails or you would like her to do her homework without being reminded, she, too, can be included in the sticker system. We provide two examples, one for school-related activities and one for home activities. (See Mike's Chart, p. 99).

This is an age group where rewards and consequences work very well. Of course, you need to use the other techniques of discipline, too. Parents should seek the help of a child psychologist while the child is in this age group. Not only will a child psychologist be there when the parents need him the most; he will also be able to work with the child when the child is most likely to be receptive to behavioral changes. During this period, parents and family still have a strong influence on the child, so it becomes very important to work on a positive self-concept for the child and work toward building positive family experiences. By all means, try the behavioral charts shown below. They can be a visual reminder of how well the child is doing, not just for the child, but for Mom and Dad, too. Using these charts with other techniques can result in a pleasant surprise. (In addition to red, blue, and gold stars, Max Kennedy received a balloon sticker when he did things without needing a reminder, and a lizard sticker when he had a great week; see Today I . . . Chart, p. 100)

Some of the techniques that work best with this age group are:

- Using systems of rewards and consequences, including charts showing token rewards.
- Allowing the child a voice in deciding a just consequence for his actions.
- Rewarding good behavior immediately.
- Providing activity-oriented rewards.
- Using time-outs.
- Having the child take responsibility for his actions.

Some things that parents will want to work on are:

- Making a disciplinary plan together.
- Being consistent in discipline.
- Being as organized as possible.
- Being very specific with rules.

Mike's Chart	M	T	W	Th	F	Sat	Sun	Leaping Lizards
Showed respect for the property of others	☆	☆			☆			
Washed hands								
Brushed teeth		☆						
Fed my dog	☆		☆	☆	☆	☆	☆	
Was nice to my sister	☆							
Shared, didn't argue		☆						
Cleaned up after myself, my toys			☆					
My bedroom								
Went to bed without a fight		☆	☆	☆	☆			

- Choosing their battles.
- Avoiding open-ended decisions.

While children in the five-to-eleven-year age group are probably in their most difficult period, they are also the most receptive. It is crucial to work with a good child psychologist during this developmental period. This is the stage in which your team members will be the most needed and the most helpful.

Twelve through Eighteen

Consequences may differ for teens, but the old system of rewards and consequences still works very well in this age group.

Today I . . .	Monday	Tuesday	Wednesday	Thursday	Friday
Did my seat work	☆	☆			
Caught the bus on time	☆	☆			
Had a fight-free recess	☆☆☆	☆			
Followed directions	☆☆☆				
Did my homework	☆				
Handed in my homework	☆				
Waited for a turn to speak	☆☆				
Stayed on task	☆	☆			

☆ Red star — I need to work on it.
☆ Blue star — I'm trying hard.
☆ Gold star — Great Job!

In fact, it is almost crucial if the parent is to maintain any kind of harmony and peace in the home. Without consequences, parents can quickly find their teenager calling the shots while they helplessly stand by, as we will see with Nora.

Handling Difficult Situations with an ADHD Teen   As a child Nora was hyperactive; as a fourteen-year-old she was calling the shots. When her parents had guests over for dinner one evening, Nora's father asked her to tell her visiting friend it was time to go home. Nora ignored her father, and when her friend asked what he had said, Nora responded, "Oh, you don't have to listen to him. You can stay." Unwilling to cause a scene, Nora's father did nothing. At one point Nora took her friend into her parents' bedroom to watch TV and Nora's mother informed them both that she did not want them in her bedroom. Again, Nora ignored her mother, saying to her friend, "Come on; we'll miss the movie." When Nora's friend turned to Nora and not Nora's parents for the final word, it became quite obvious that discipline had broken down totally.

During her childhood, Nora's parents never worked out a disciplinary plan, and worse yet, they were divided in their approach to discipline with Nora. How should her parents have handled the situation?

When Nora told her friend she did not have to go home, Dad should have stepped in and told her friend, "I'm sorry; Nora seems to be having some difficulty understanding the rules this evening. I'm afraid you will have to go home now. You're welcome to come back another time." Then Nora should have faced a consequence: no friends over for a week. Situations like this are totally avoided when parents have raised hyperactive children with disciplinary plans on which they agree. The child has learned long ago that Mom and Dad mean what they say and say what they mean.

Discipline for teens still includes the same need for praise and rewards for good behavior, but do not be afraid to take away the car keys, curtail activities, or remove privileges. Some of the old techniques will not work on teens (sticker charts, et cetera), but rewards and consequences work quite well with teens.

Contracting is another successful management technique. All teenagers like to express their independence. They do not want you to "run" their lives. Sometimes they do not want parents to tell them what time to get in or what they can and cannot do. While teens need to express their views on topics, you have to remember a teenager is not an adult yet. He is not ready to run his own life yet. He still requires monitoring.

When you reach a real impasse with a teenager, a contract may be the best solution. Sit down with your teenager and draw up a contract. Spell out what the rules are, what you expect him to do, what he expects from you, and what the consequences and rewards are. You will need to negotiate some issues. A simple contract could look like this:

> Danny Jones will be paid for all chores he does around the house when they are completed. He will come home from school every day and do two hours of homework per evening before returning to school to watch basketball games. He will inform his parents who he is with and where he is at all times.
>
> His parents, Bill and Mary Jones, will not go into his room without Dan's permission. Dan will be allowed to have his friends over if he checks it out with his parents first. Dan can go to as many basketball games as he wants to if he does his homework first.

You will want to spell out the consequence, and both parents and children will need to sign the contract. Putting it in writing is important. Then it is down in black and white for parent and child to remember the agreement.

Perhaps the most important part of disciplining a hyperactive child is learning to discipline yourself. It takes enormous amounts of parental time and energy always to be consistent, to organize everything, to intervene instead of react, and to keep things positive. Parents have to discipline themselves to stick to the rules and not give in to a child who can be demanding, manipulative, difficult, and persistent. While it may be easier to give in today, you will pay a higher price tomorrow. The results of good discipline, like giving in, are not always seen the same day or even the same week, but these techniques do work. Good discipline techniques will help your child to achieve, to feel good about himself, and to fit into his world more comfortably. The time you invest in appropriate discipline today will pay off tomorrow in fewer temper tantrums, better social behavior, and a better family life for everyone.

CHAPTER 7

Siblings and Family and Friends

Siblings

Almost everyone understands that raising a hyperactive child is difficult. What our families and friends do not always understand is that raising other children in a family with a special child is also difficult. Having to raise a "normal" child along with your ADHD child presents its own set of challenges most parents never face. Parents are not the only people who find living with a hyperactive child a challenge; so do the siblings.

Brothers and sisters of hyperactive children are normal children who do not live normal lives. Frequently they feel they have to hide their toys and/or other belongings to keep them safe from a hyperactive sibling. They are reluctant to have friends over because often the hyperactive child will "horn in" on their play and, after joining uninvited, will cause a scene or a fight. They may find they dislike their hyperactive sibling because of his behavior and feel guilty, a double whammy. Usually they resent the time, energy, and attention they see their parents concentrating on this "needy" child when they know the parents' attention and time would normally be divided equally. Often they feel their sibling has life easier than they do. Almost always they feel their life is unfair: Their parents have higher expectations for them than their "special sibling," and the sibling "gets away with a lot more."

Last fall Karen went trick-or-treating with her ADHD brother, Johnny. Johnny ate all of his candy the first day, got sick, and threw up. Two days later, he saw Karen's candy on the dining room table and ate all of her candy, too. Here's what happened.

KAREN: Mom, Johnny ate all of my candy. I hate him. It's not fair. He ate his candy, and he ate mine, too. Punish him, Mom. He deserves it.

MOM: No, it wasn't fair. I'm sure Johnny didn't think before he did it. Johnny has a handicap. What do you think is a fair thing to do?

KAREN: I think he should pay me twenty dollars, do all my work for six months, and buy me new Halloween candy.

MOM: Well, it's a good idea for him to pay you back. How about a penny per piece of candy? Or you could have him use his money to buy you a bag of candy you like. How about chocolate kisses?

In this case Mom did some things to make life more pleasant for the other child in the family. In the following pages we will analyze these techniques and some others you will find useful.

Explain

You will want to explain to your other child that his brother or sister has a disability.

MOM: I know you are angry. You walked a long time for that Halloween candy on a cold night. But you need to know Johnny's brain works a little differently than yours and mine. He doesn't always think before he acts. That's why he ate all of your Halloween candy, and now he's sorry. He didn't stop and think about it until it was too late. I am sure that Johnny would like to be like you. No one wants to have other people mad at them, but his brain does not always click in and let him think before he acts.

In this example, Mom gave Johnny's sister two very important facts: Johnny has a disability, and Johnny would not have done it if he had a choice. Knowing this is not going to bring back the candy, and Johnny's sister is still going to feel things are not fair. You may want Johnny to pay his sister one or two cents for each piece of candy he ate. There is a possibility the sister knows exactly how many pieces of candy are missing and is ready for compensation. However, the explanation is still important, because understanding goes a long way toward tolerance.

As a parent, you know life with the ADHD child is not easy, and it helps to have someone to talk to who understands. You will want to encourage your normal child to talk with you about his feelings without making him feel guilty.

Make Rules Everyone Can Live With

One of the things that makes living with a hyperactive child difficult is the necessity to change your parenting style. This child requires more structure than other children. Often parents will say how much it hurts them to be so strict. They would prefer to parent in a more relaxed style that is not possible with their ADHD child. With most children it is not necessary to be so specific or have a rule for almost every occasion. With a hyperactive child it is. Privileges and rights can be further complicated by the ADHD child's position in the family: Is he the oldest, youngest, or middle child? Privileges and responsibilities that would normally be given to the oldest child may be inappropriate when the oldest child has this handicap. Most parents find it difficult to make rules that are not necessary for their "normal" children but seem to be for the ADHD child. So, how do we make rules that are fair to everyone?

- Make skill-based rules, not age-based rules. Tell your hyperactive child he can ride a two-wheel bicycle when his balance is good enough, not when he is six years old, or he can get his driver's license when he has proved he can maintain a C+ average, not just when he is sixteen.
- Have the same rules for everyone. If you have to pay your hyperactive child immediately for jobs because he cannot delay gratification, you will have to pay your other children right away, too, even though they can delay gratification.
- Make sure all children know what the rules are. Children, even the ones who are not hyperactive, try to claim ignorance of the law. Explanations made before the fact eliminate the problem.
- Live by the rules yourself. If you have a rule like "No phone calls after 9:30 P.M.," then you should make a point of not making calls after that time either.
- If at all possible, discuss problems before making rules. Giving the children, including the hyperactive child, a voice in making the rules will make it easier for them to follow those rules.

Reward Your "Normal" Children for Their Capabilities

Many times the other siblings will feel the hyperactive child does not have to do as much as they do. In all probability this is true, because sometimes it is necessary to give the hyperactive child less work. One child made a point of telling her mother she felt her ADHD brother had life pretty easy because the mother made his lunch for him throughout elementary school and junior high, while she, two years younger, always made her own lunch.

MARY: It's not fair, Mom. You favor Johnny. You always make his lunch, but I have to buy mine or make it myself.

MOM: You know, Mary, you're right. I probably should make your lunch for you, but I don't have time in the morning. I'll tell you what. I could either make your lunch for you the night before or we could go out to lunch once a week on Saturday. I'll let you choose.

Of course this happened because the hyperactive child could barely manage to get himself fed, dressed, collected, and out the door each morning. Recognizing the other child's legitimate feelings of being slighted, the mother offered two solutions. She offered to either make lunches for both children the night before or take her daughter out to lunch every Saturday afternoon, just the two of them, as a reward for her helping out by making one of the lunches. The daughter chose Saturday lunch with Mom.

There are lots of little things our "normal" children do we take for granted, like making their own lunch. It is important to notice these accomplishments and to reward them for the little things they do on their own, even if you do nothing more than take them out for a hamburger once a week.

Give Them Time with Their Friends without the ADHD Child Around

One of the biggest complaints of siblings of a hyperactive children is that their brother or sister makes it hard for them to play with their friends. If you can, try to arrange for a day a month when your other children can have their friends over to play while the hyperactive child is away from home. Use the opportunities like music lessons or soccer practice or even a visit from Grandma. If you have to, hire a sitter to take your hyperactive child out for two hours a month so your other children can have friends over. It may not seem like a lot, but it gives that child a few hours of relief, while it gives the ADHD child some one-on-one attention, too.

Provide a Safe Place

Another common complaint of siblings is that nothing is "safe" from their ADHD sibling. They know all too well their impulsive sibling takes things without asking, sometimes breaking belongings or using them all, like Goldilocks.

If each child has his own room, then that room should become the safe place. Most hyperactive children can learn not to go into anyone else's room without permission. If your child has to share a room with an ADHD child, you will need to find a separate place for him to store special items he does not want to share.

Teach the Hyperactive Child Respect for Property

Trying to teach a hyperactive child respect for other people's property can be difficult. Sometimes it involves rules like: "Do not go into someone's bedroom without knocking and waiting for permission." Siblings of hyperactive children need to have a safe place to put their belongings, and their own rooms seem to be the logical choice.

Now that you have made the rule to respect the privacy and sanctity of all family members, how are you going to get your impulsive child to comply? This is what the Kennedys did.

> For us, Post-its worked very well. We bought a stack of them in lots of colors. We used these as a flag of sorts, a visual reminder, to give us that one second it takes to stop an impulsive act and make the child stop and think. Because you want the child to stop, red or bright pink ones work very well. By cutting the corners off, the Post-it

looked even more like a stop sign. We wrote little messages on these "stop" signs like "Mom's drawer, ask first," "Meggie's room, keep out," or even, "Close door."

You will want to keep messages on these "stop" signs short and pointed. You will also want to put them at the eye level of your impulsive child, where he cannot miss them. While these are not the only answer, they are one visual tool to break the impulsivity and allow the child to stop and think.

Set Aside Time for Your Other Children, Too

Just as you need to spend one-on-one time with your hyperactive child and your husband, you'll need to put aside time for your other child or children. Brothers and sisters of ADHD children suffer many of the same strains their parents do, so offer them the same praise and positive rewards of your time you give to your hyperactive child. There are always the special events like Mom's Day at school or Blue and Gold Parent's Banquet at Scouts, but try to schedule special time when you can do something with your other child on a weekly basis. The Kennedys used "special time" as a reward for all of the helpful things their daughter did. Sometimes it was little more than taking her shopping to pick out a new Barbie doll dress she had earned or her dad taking her to a gymnastics meet. Special time was her time, when she had her parents all to herself, without interruptions, without her sibling.

Teach Them Coping Skills, Too

Just as you have worked on coping skills with your hyperactive child, you will want to work on coping skills with your "normal" child. This child needs to learn:

- To handle frustration, using outside interests, social skills, exercise, and support from friends and family.
- To understand his brother's disability of hyperactivity.

- To express himself verbally (when he is old enough, role-playing is a helpful way to express his feelings).
- To resist feelings of guilt about or responsibility for his hyperactive sibling.
- To treat his sibling with respect and kindness.

Family and Friends

Other family members and friends may also have a difficult time coping with the ADHD child. Like the brothers and sisters of these children, the grandparents may suffer some of the same problems your children do. Many times they dislike the way your hyperactive child behaves, but rather than face the guilt as grandparents who do not like their grandchild, they blame you for not doing a good job raising this child.

Give Your Parents an Explanation of Hyperactivity

Be sure to tell them it is not caused by bad parenting. Your child is different. Tell them hyperactive children, even ones you have not raised, have the same set of problems in common: impulsivity, restlessness, and difficulty paying attention.

Tell them you are working on behavior management with your child. Share with them the techniques you use to build self-esteem and encourage them to do the same when they are with your child. Grandparents need to understand these are special children and they require special parenting techniques. Some of the old ways of parenting they used on you simply will not work on this child. Unless your parents have a good understanding of hyperactivity and are quite accepting, it is best to share successes and save the setbacks for your friends or support group.

Developing Friendships

TEACHING RESPECT FOR THE HYPERACTIVE CHILD

ADHD children are often able to identify with Rodney Dangerfield when he says, "I get no respect." Gaining the respect of other children is very difficult for ADHD children. They are constantly getting in trouble and constantly causing trouble for other children. On any given day, someone, somewhere, is usually mad at the ADHD child for something.

How can you help him to gain the respect of his classmates?

- Encourage him in an area where he is very good. Sometimes this is a musical instrument, sometimes it's computer games, and sometimes it's sports. Whatever he is good at, encourage it, especially if it's an activity that can be done with other children, family or friends. This develops respect for the child in skills he *has* mastered.
- Have other children over when you have the time to supervise closely. Keeping your hyperactive child's needs in mind, you will want to plan games and activities. Remember, these children grow mentally tired of the same activity after twenty to thirty minutes unless it is something new and exciting, so you will want to plan activities accordingly. Plan activities your child is good at and has shown some interest in. You want his friends to see him as a good playmate, not as someone who gives up right away.

Helping Friendships Along

Most children make friends easily. For hyperactive children forming and keeping friendships is anything but easy. ADHD children miss the social cues other children pick up so easily. They lack the little social skills that are needed. If a parent is there, the adult can remind the child to "take turns" or "do not grab; wait until your friend is through." But there will be times when the parent cannot be there. There are some things parents can do to help.

When the children are younger, four to ten years old, parents have some say about the friends with whom their children chose to play. You can help direct your child toward other children who have similar interests: Lego blocks, playing soccer, or catching tadpoles. Some activities, like catching tadpoles, can remain unstructured, and the hyperactive child can do fairly well in an activity with that much variety involved in it. Other activities, like building a tree fort, doing a cooking project, or playing a computer game, may require more planning. Once your child's friend is there, you will want to sit down with them and make sure the play goes smoothly.

- Have them talk about the rules. The adult may want to write them down so the child has a visual reminder: "We can mix the cookies, roll them out, and use the cookie cutters, but only Mom can put them in the oven and take them out." Write in turns to be taken: "Max gets to make twenty cookies; Jenny gets to make twenty cookies. Then we can eat them." Is there cleanup? Plan that, too: "Max will wash dishes; Jenny will dry the dishes; Mom will put dishes away and wipe off the counter."
- Have them make a plan. The younger they are, the simpler the plans will be, but they should know what they plan to do, where they plan to do it, and for how long: "We will make the cookies at the counter in the kitchen, not on the living room floor, and Jenny will be here for two hours, so it will take about that long. Then we eat them."

While outside activities require less planning than inside activities, you will still want the children to take time to think some of this out. Again, this is a way to control some of the impulsive behavior that causes so much trouble.

PLAN AHEAD AS MUCH AS POSSIBLE

Parents of hyperactive children usually find they are the ones who have to have other children over. Whether this is because

ADHD children are not the at the top of the popularity polls or their friends' parents are not wild about having overactive children over, the fact remains that most of the action will occur in your home. Of course the disadvantage to this is that you and your family could use the break, while the advantage is that your child has a better chance of a successful play experience with you in control. Should your child be invited to someone else's home, by all means tell the parents he will do better outside and that he will do better if there is a lot of variety in the activity. If it is something new, all the better, and some planning is required.

Even situations that seem harmless can turn into social disasters if parents do not plan ahead very carefully. This is an example of what happened to John on a Boy Scout trip.

Avoiding Turmoil in the Teen Years

At thirteen, John had worked hard to keep up with the other boys in his Boy Scout troop. He was a good swimmer and enjoyed the practice that was required for a fifty-mile overnight canoe trip. A key part of the practice was a canoe safety and survival lesson. The boys needed to learn basics of boating safety rules and to demonstrate in an actual simulated situation that they could right a swamped and overturned canoe. John passed the simulated test in the gym. He would have less luck on the river.

Friday, after school, the group of twelve boys and four adult leaders left for a camping site about seventy miles south of Portland, Oregon. After the boys had set up their tents, they began to prepare their individual meals. All had brought along pots, pans, and individual camping stoves for the two-day trip—all, that is, except John. Although he had looked forward to this trip, John had forgotten to bring cooking utensils. He had brought hamburger meat and rolls for lunch and dinner and pancake mix for breakfast. He asked Bill, a fellow scout, if he could use his frying pan.

"Sure, no problem. I made some burgers myself. My stove is still on. Go ahead and use it."

The frying pan had about two ounces of warm—and quite liquid—fat from Bill's lunch. John looked at the grease in the pan, then briefly looked around. How could he get rid of it? Without a moment's thought John took the lower portion of his new jacket and wiped the frying pan clean.

"Oh, God," one of the scouts said. "Look what John did *this* time! Can you believe it?"

It would have taken John perhaps forty-five seconds to have cleaned his borrowed frying pan correctly. That was too long for John. He was beginning to compound errors.

The next morning John woke up and again looked helpless. He had a bag of pancake mix, but no bowl to mix it in, no frying pan, no stove, and no utensils. He was too embarrassed after the night before to ask Bill again. He "borrowed" a pan without asking, then scooped in pancake mix and water without measuring. He had nothing to stir it with, so he looked around and in an instant picked up part of an expensive Swedish stove. Without asking, he used it to stir his pancake mix.

"John," said Henry, "what are you doing with that? That is the fuel regulator for my Primus stove. How could you use that to stir your pancakes?"

This time it was not John's mother or father who was angry. It was not his teacher, the bus driver, or the school principle. It was a fellow scout who was angry and upset about such a completely careless and impulsive act.

John had gotten into trouble already, and the canoes had not yet been placed in the Willamette River for the fifty-mile trip. On the canoe trip, John was positioned in the center of a three-person canoe. An experienced fourteen-year-old scout controlled the canoe from the stern, and an adult leader assisted from the front of the canoe. After two hours of paddling they and the other canoeists brought their canoes toward shore to get on solid ground and stretch their legs. John "forgot" one of the safety rules. He stood up before the canoe was secure. He climbed on the side of the canoe and jumped ashore, tipping over the canoe, spilling the other two and all the gear into the river.

Later in the day, while John was minding his business and no scout leader was present, two scouts beat up John. It was a "get even" fight to teach John "a lesson." John had many such "lessons."

The trip was salvaged by the adult leaders working out a plan in which an adult was assigned to John for the remainder of the trip.

How Could Planning Have Helped?

What could have been done to spare John and his fellow scouts from this experience?

First, John's parents should have seen to it that John made a list of all the equipment he needed. While it was John's responsibility to gather the equipment, his parents have to recognize the fact that ADHD children need monitoring. A list is one way to help them learn to "check" on themselves. Monitoring, right up to the point where Mom makes sure John's equipment is in the van, is necessary for ADHD children and teens.

Second, John's parents should have been aware that he would require more adult supervision than most and then made sure there were enough adults to handle the situation, even if it meant they had to volunteer in order to make it a successful experience for John. If someone from the family could not volunteer, then by all means someone should meet with the adult leaders ahead of time and clue them in, telling them the child acts impulsively and doesn't pay attention so he needs to be reminded of the rules, giving them ideas on how to handle John if and when difficult situations come up, and letting them know if John was on medication and when it should be taken.

Third, if at all possible, John's parents should have tried to find a good "match" between the troop (or group) and John. A troop that has other children with handicaps or one that has leaders with special training is helpful. Sometimes a church group with understanding youth leaders (teens who assist the adult leaders) can work well.

PART 3

How to Advocate for your Child

Dealing with the Schools

How to Work with the Schools

Schools are a crucial part of the equation that determines how well your hyperactive child succeeds. ADHD children face most of their problems with both attention deficit and hyperactivity in school. At school they have to listen, sit at a desk, and behave "appropriately." At home they can get up and walk around when they hit their attention span limit; they can do something physical outside, or they can talk whenever they want. Schools can produce their biggest problems and their biggest failures and play a major role in the ultimate success of the child. The key is making sure the school, the teacher, or someone at the school is part of the team.

What Kinds of Problems Arise

Problems at school fall into two categories: behavioral problems and academic problems. Schools can provide information that is vital for diagnosis of ADHD and learning disabilities. Also, they can provide physicians and parents with feedback that is needed for them to decide what direction to take with the child and how well the current programs are working. While parent, teacher, and child psychologist may all be working on academic and behavioral problems, for much of the day teacher and child will have to work on them together. Not only is it preferable; it is vital that the teacher be part of the team.

Some Solutions

More than anything, good communication with the schools will go the furthest and produce the best results in resolving educational problems with your child. You will need more than the regularly scheduled monthly or quarterly progress reports schools have for all students. For best results frequent, day-to-day communication with the classroom teacher is necessary for elementary-aged children. But day-to-day conferences sound overwhelming to teachers who are overworked and stressed out already.

Once again, you will want to analyze your goals. What is the information you really need to know every day? In elementary school you may need daily reports, while junior high or middle school may require biweekly to weekly reports and high school work may require weekly to bimonthly reports. More than likely you need to know how your child has done and when he is in trouble *before* the situation is totally out of control.

- Has he finished his assignments?
- Has he stayed on-task?
- Has he waited his turn?
- Has he turned in assignments?

To be successful in your behavior management program, you need to know how your child performs in school so you can intervene before things get out of hand.

Stick-ums or Post-it notepads are a simple and effective way for teachers to communicate with parents on a daily basis. Parents can buy stick-um pads with smiley faces and sad faces to give to the teacher for their child to use. Three pads of forty stick-ums with smiley faces and two pads with sad faces should last you an entire school year. If you cannot find smiley face stick-ums, use a plain pad and a smiley face stamp. On the cardboard back you can list reasons for a sad face:

1. Did not finish work
2. Did not stay on-task, et cetera

If you cannot afford stick-ums, you can take a sheet of paper and draw eight squares with smiley faces and have it photocopied. At three cents a page, it will cost less than fifty cents. While this may sound like a little bit of work, it is important that the parents do the work and ask nothing more of the teacher than that he send home either a happy or sad face each day with a note indicating the corresponding reason why the child had a bad day or a good day at school.

Parent and teacher may want to work together on giving the child shorter assignments in school and allowing the child to complete written work on the computer. The level of work is not the problem for these children; the amount of work is. Since these children suffer mental fatigue more rapidly than normal children, completing huge amounts of work will be difficult for them. Parents and teachers can provide some relief from the mental fatigue by having the child use a computer. Some basic features of the computer—visual images, immediate feedback, and frequent feedback—make it an ideal learning tool for the hyperactive child. Any schoolwork that can be done on the computer should be.

Token systems that work so well in improving behavior and education for these kids also require communication between home and school, as does progress on behavioral charts. Dr. Russell Barkley stated:

Token systems are to the hyperactive child what a wheelchair is to the crippled child. It is not a question of "if" we should use a token system with the child in the classroom; it is a must.[1]

Just as a behavior chart is very important at home, it is equally, if not more, important in the classroom. However, teachers may not want to take the time or effort to make one out for your child. They are reluctant to treat any child in a special way. You will have to point out to them that this is a necessity for this type of handicap.

You will have to take some of the responsibility. Teachers are far more cooperative if someone hands them the supplies needed for a token system and says, "We're using a token system at home with Max, and we find it very successful. He has to have one in the classroom, too, so we can both work toward improving his behavior in class and at home." Most teachers will be more than happy to cooperate. Be sure to keep track of how long the tokens or charts should last so you have enough "rewards." Changing tokens or rewards is also important. Remember, hyperactive children grow tired of the same tokens week after week and will not work for them after a while, so rotate your tokens. Check with the teacher from time to time on your child's progress. After all, they have an interest in seeing an improvement in your child's behavior, too.

Some teachers use team charts for the whole class, showing class progress in various areas. Having the added benefit of working with classmates may prove even better for your child. Consider buying inexpensive cardboard puzzles and giving puzzle pieces as tokens. Not only does this involve other class members in the project; it also promotes cooperation between the hyperactive child and his classmates, who will work together on the puzzle.

Working with the Preschool Hyperactive Child

It is sometime during the preschool years that many parents first suspect that their child is hyperactive. For this reason, few parents of hyperactive children need encouragement to put their child in preschool. Parents may see it as a much needed respite from the endless motion and commotion; they should also see it as a head start on the school situation. Preschools offer an opportunity for the child to grow socially, emotionally, and intellectually, but for parents they can offer something even more valuable: early detection of learning disabilities. For these reasons choosing a nursery school is very important.

What Should Parents Look for in a Preschool?

The school should be willing to let you, as a prospective parent, observe and interview the staff about their philosophy and methods at their school. The administrators should be willing to share the educational backgrounds of staff members. You can feel fairly confident in teachers with backgrounds in early childhood education, child psychology, or elementary education. Ask if you may observe the teachers interacting with the children. You will want to observe in a quiet corner away from the action, being careful not to interact with the children yourself.

If we start with the physical layout of the nursery school, one of the most important things parents should look for is an outdoor play area. Hyperactive children frequently need redirection to appropriate outdoor play: i.e., "Johnny, we need to throw balls, not blocks. You can throw the balls outside, where the wooden clown makes a better target than Sarah." Redirection and learning social skills is difficult, if not impossible, without a large outdoor play area. In the outdoor area you will want to look for equipment available to exercise the large muscles: swings, climbing equipment, a sandbox or garden area to dig in, and tricycles to ride. You will want to look for a portion of the outdoor area that is covered, allowing outdoor play during inclement weather. Keep in mind that hyperactive children do best with exercise that uses muscles without getting them overly excited. One-on-one games are better than team games that have lots of running, tagging, or jumping or games that are heavy on the chaos and light on structure. Swinging, jumping rope, and playing hopscotch are all better for a hyperactive child than playing tag or dodgeball.

The indoor physical layout should include a large area where children can move freely from one activity to another and a small quiet corner where a child can get away from it all. Indoor activities usually help develop fine-muscle skills: painting, drawing, coloring, playing with Play-Doh, cutting and pasting, or doing a number of art activities. Some indoor activities like the house corner and the story corner develop social skills and learning and listening skills. In some nursery schools the "circle" corner is called the quiet corner, but often hyperactive children will need somewhere where they can get away from the large group within the room, even if it is nothing more than a hallway leading into the room.

Parents should be prepared to ask the teachers and staff some important questions: "Do you have a schedule that you follow every day?" Hyperactive children need structure, a predictable pattern to follow, but there has to be some flexibility within that structure. Hyperactive children need to know what is coming next. A school that offers free play from 9:00 to 10:30, ten minutes of cleanup, followed by forty minutes of story and circle time, may sound fine, but will require more investigation. During free play are the children allowed a variety of activities, such as painting, block building, Play-Doh, house corner, and outside play? Is there any time limit on how much time a child can spend doing a given activity? The hyperactive child may spend two minutes painting, ten minutes playing with building blocks, and all the rest of his time outside. This will work out well for the hyperactive child, but there are other things you will want to consider.

A well-educated teacher should check each child's fine-motor skills, eye-hand coordination, and tracking skills (how well his eyes follow an activity or motion). Skills, or lack of skills, involved in coloring, drawing, cutting paper, and throwing a ball and catching it can indicate possible learning difficulties. Sooner or later most children will attempt some or all of these activities. A talented teacher will take time to observe the child and check his skill level without being demanding.

Problems arise when the school has a rigid schedule, saying, for example, every child has to work on painting, blocks, an art project, and Play-Doh each and every day. They may allow the child to choose when he wants to do these activities, but they require each child to do each activity every day and for no more than ten minutes a day. Ten minutes of outside play is not always enough for an ADHD child, and ten minutes in the house corner is probably nine minutes too much.

Circle and story time can prove especially difficult for the hyperactive child. Parents will want to ask the teacher what her goals for story time are. If the goal is to teach listening skills, she may want to consider alternatives to circle time for the hyperactive child. Hopefully, there will be a teacher and an aide or parent helper at the school. While at some schools the teacher will read the story and an aide will sit in a circle with the more rambunctious children, hyperactive children will get the most out of this "group time" if the aide takes them out of the circle immediately after sharing time and takes them to a quiet corner, reading to them on a one-on-one basis. If the teacher's goals for group time are learning, listening or auditory skills, and learning to take turns, then this is almost a necessity.

Group time, with its many distractions, makes the development of listening skills almost impossible for the ADHD child. Hyperactive children can do better in smaller groups, where they will not get as wound up and do not have so much to filter out. They respond better in one-on-one situations.

This brings us to another very important question you will want to ask. What is the teacher-student ratio? The closer you can get to a one-to-five teacher-student ratio, the better. Most nursery schools have one-to-ten. You will want to see if the school allows volunteers. You will want to ask how thoroughly they screen teachers and volunteers, not just for the standard measures of safety, but for their flexibility and understanding. Do not be afraid to ask teachers how they would handle a situation you know your child has been in or created:

Mrs. Jones, what would you do if a child knocked over another child's block building while running through the block corner?

A well-educated teacher will use redirection: "We tell the children they may run outside, but not in the block corner, and we ask them to help rebuild the structure with the child who created it." A good teacher will make sure the child who knocked over the blocks understands the problem his actions created for the other child and work to remedy them. This builds understanding for the feelings of other children, a concept hyperactive children sometimes have a hard time grasping.

More punitive teachers may react differently:

> When children knock down someone's blocks because they disobeyed the rules on running we make them sit in the corner for ten minutes, then pick up all the blocks at cleanup time.

The teacher in the first example will give your child a positive preschool experience and help the child to grow and develop socially, while the teacher in the second example will not.

Working with the Elementary-School–Aged Hyperactive Child

With any luck your child will have a wonderful kindergarten teacher. He will pick up on any areas of concern: coordination, speech and hearing difficulties, perceptual problems, and other possible learning disabilities. Regardless of his ability as a teacher, you will want to go in and talk to him in the beginning of the year and tell him your concerns so he can watch your child to either verify or put your concerns to rest. The teacher and the parent are two parts of the team that must work together daily, so make contact with the teacher at the earliest possible time. Hyperactive children do better if their desk is closer to the teacher and the front of the room. You will want to go in and tell the teacher this before he makes out his seating chart, so use the opportunity as a chance to get to know him and start a working relationship.

In some ways the structure and scheduling of most elementary schools will help your child function; in other ways it will cause problems. In many classrooms, teachers will assign board work (work placed on the chalkboard) for children to do while they take a small, skill-divided group to read. It is the board work and writing work, as well as work done in workbooks, that can cause problems for the hyperactive child. Both require the child to pay attention, listen to instructions, and work at a self-directed pace. Hyperactive children need supervision and visual reminders of tasks and rules. Have the teacher's aide write the task out on a three-by-five card for the child. This way he can refer back to a visual confirmation of instructions and does not have to rely on verbal memory. This is often helpful. Self-direction is a skill that will take a long while for these children to develop.

Encourage the teacher to schedule your child's hardest subjects in the morning, when he is freshest. A hyperactive child with a mild learning disability that is causing some delay in reading is not going to learn to read if he is going off to the reading lab at two o'clock every afternoon.

Be sure to share with your child's teacher what you know about your child. Once Pat Kennedy told a teacher that her son had better attention after he had a brief period of physical activity. The next day the teacher shared something with Pat Kennedy. It had to be one-on-one or solitary physical activity. Playing flag ball wound him up higher than a kite. The teacher was right. From then on the teacher kept Max's "physical activities" to swinging, catch, hopscotch, balance beam, and other nongroup or small-group activities. While physical activity is important to ADHD children, the chaos of large team sports can be very difficult for them, especially the elementary-grade children. Some ADHD children will have difficulty "switching attention" or coming down from a high level of physical activity to a quieter indoor activity. The parent and the teacher will have to work together to find out when an ADHD child has optimal attention.

Sometimes how well an ADHD child does during the school year is completely dependent on a single factor: who his teacher is. Yet as parents of hyperactive children we feel as though we are always in the principal's office. Frequently parents are made to feel as if they owe the school an apology for sending them their less-than-perfect child. No wonder parents are hesitant to request a specific teacher for their child. At best schools discourage requests for teachers, and some actually forbid it, yet it is very important to an ADHD child's and his parents' well-being that he be given the right teacher.

So, what is the best way to request a teacher without requesting? First, go in and talk to a teacher who knows your child and has had some measure of success with him. Ask this teacher who of the possible teachers your child may get would handle his specific problems the best. Your next step should be to set up an appointment with the principal. Do not request a specific teacher, but *do* request specific qualities in a teacher. You might want to say something like this:

Thank you for seeing me, Mr. Smith. I know the end of the school year is a busy time, but I thought we needed to get together and go over Max's progress. As you know, he did very well with Mrs. Jones, but he kind of fell apart the three weeks the student teacher was there. I am not going to request a specific teacher, but I think it is obvious that things can get pretty bad if Max has a teacher that does not have certain skills. I have made a list of teaching qualities that I feel are necessary for Max to function in the classroom, and I would like to go over them with you.

At this point a parent will want to be fully prepared with a list of teaching skills necessary for success with a hyperactive child.

Max needs a teacher who is very organized and follows a pattern or schedule. He needs someone who writes down the steps or directions either on the chalk board or on paper for the children to follow in addition to telling them [the multiple sensory approach to learning]. Because hyperactive children do not always catch just auditory instructions, Max will also need to be able to look back at the written instructions when he is distracted.

Max needs a teacher who is structured but not rigid. He needs someone who will not hold him back in math because his coordination problems prevent him from completing timed tests. He needs someone who is willing to let him get up and move around after he has been sitting for fifteen minutes, because fifteen minutes is as long as he can sit. He needs someone who is willing to use a token system with him. He needs a teacher who believes in hands-on learning, who is animated and interesting. And most of all, he needs someone who is willing to be part of Max's team and work with us, our pediatrician and child psychologist.

If his previous teacher suggested a teacher he feels would work well with your child, by all means throw in some of that teacher's specific characteristics.

"I feel a male teacher would be very good for him right now," or "he needs a woman teacher right now because he needs some extra mothering," or "he needs a teacher who has good social skills and can help him feel as though he's part of a group and help the group appreciate his special talents."

Make sure you discuss your goals with the principal, what you feel your child needs to accomplish next year. Tell him you want a teacher who can help your child achieve those goals.

Requesting teacher qualities instead of a specific teacher has another highly recommendable benefit: It puts the responsibility squarely on the principal. After a few weeks, if you find your child assigned to a teacher who looks like a disaster for your child, you will have every right to go in and request that he be moved. The principal is far more likely to correct his error than yours.

Working with the Junior-High–Aged Hyperactive Child

In school, you will want to make sure your child is getting the help he needs in areas where he is deficient and advancing in the areas where he excels. If he plays a mean trumpet, make sure they allow him in band, or if he is a computer whiz, make sure he is allowed to take computer classes. Sometimes his hyperactivity will make teachers reluctant to put him in the "extra" classes, but be insistent. It is important that the child meet with not only success, but recognition from his peers. Being a good goalie for the soccer team can go a long way toward strengthening friendships for a child who has difficulty keeping friends.

New situations at school also produce stress for the ADHD youngster. For the first time, more demands are made on him. He has to change classes, adjust to four or five teachers instead of one, and remember a locker combination. All of these new experiences require organization and social skills. To a preteen it can seem overwhelming.

By the time your child is in junior high, hopefully all of his learning disabilities will be identified. While some children, already in a learning center setting, will need to stay there, it is important to make sure your child is mainstreamed where and when it is at all possible. It is important to keep in mind that hyperactive children frequently have multiple disabilities and they should always be diagnosed and treated as early as possible. This becomes even more important as the child enters junior high. If you suspect the schools or physicians have overlooked a possible disability, by all means have a team check it out.

Junior high students face increased demands in terms of written work, homework, and other assignments from not one teacher, but at least three or four. As we said before, written work can be very difficult for ADHD children. A meeting early in the school year with the child psychologist, parents, and all of the teachers can go a long way toward working out goals and solutions for your child. Some of the teachers may be willing to let your child take taped "notes" or take his tests verbally, while other teachers may be willing to let him do most of his work on the computer. Do not be upset if not all teachers are equally cooperative. If two of the four teachers are willing to let your child tape reports or take a test verbally, you are still ahead of the game.

Working with the Hyperactive High-School–Aged Student

Working with high school hyperactive children presents its own problems and solutions. Here again, you will want to make sure you identify all academic strengths and weaknesses. Once in high school, many hyperactive children find they need to spend an hour or two a day in the learning center and are mainstreamed for the rest of the day.

For the slower learner or the learning-disabled, high school can prove frustrating. Sometimes these children do better in alternative classes. You may want to look into vocational classes or other classes that help develop skills that can be used for employment.

Impulsivity is still a problem for the high school student, but by now he may have more skills to deal with his problems. Junior high and high school students can learn to curb impulsive tendencies with the old "reporter" technique. Before you do something, think about who, what, when, where, how, and why.

- Who is going to do this?

  Me, Kara, the sophomore.

- What?

  I am going to cook Chinese food for my world studies class and get an A.

- When?

  Tomorrow.

- Where?

  In my second period class in world studies.

- How?

  Here the child needs to show some planning: "Mom is going to buy the food. I am going to take a pan and a hot plate."

- Why?

  So I can get an A by showing the teacher how much I know about what people in China grow and eat.

Actually, this is a pretty good project for a hyperactive child; it is hands-on and active, and the report can be given verbally. Mom needs to ask some questions to help Kara fill in the gaps. "You said you wanted me to buy the food, but it is your project. When would you like to go shopping with me to buy the food? How are you going to serve it? And let me hear your speech on the crops and diets of China." When parents ask the who, what, when, where, how, why and how much questions, they invite the child to do some planning and take more responsibility.

Social skills remain a problem for most hyperactive children throughout high school, yet most teens will resist social skills classes as "retarded." Ask your guidance counselor about the possibility of indirect teaching of social skills by using carefully chosen teachers and classes. Bright children really enjoy psychology, debate, personal relation, or family life classes. Many of these classes stress working as a team, role-playing, expressing feelings, and learning to listen to someone else's feelings. ADHD children can learn as many, if not more, social skills from these classes as they can from the more direct methods used in a social skills class. Whether you opt for the social skills class or the more indirect method, you will want to make the decision with your team, pediatrician, teacher/counselor, and child psychologist.

Because of the extreme emotional turmoil of the teen years, you will want to listen carefully to your hyperactive child, not just his words, but what he does as well. For example, Beth, who is always energetic, suddenly becomes lethargic. She does not want to do her favorite activities, and all she wants to do is sleep. She may say negative things like: "No one likes me," or "I am not pretty enough." As a parent you will want to look into this right away. Try to get her to open up, if not to you then to her psychologist or a teacher. Mild and severe depressions can be caused by many things: trouble with a course in school, liking a member of the opposite sex and not having the social skills to handle it, and, common to all teens, ADHD or not, trying to find a niche, a peer group where he is accepted.

If you have worked with a team all along, then the established relationship with the child psychologist will be very beneficial during these years. Do not be afraid to seek help at the first signs of depression or other forms of emotional difficulties with your hyperactive child.

For the most part schools are willing to work with parents and the team to help their child succeed. If your child has pure ADD or ADHD without additional complicating factors like coordination problems or learning disabilities, you are lucky. However, you may also be at a disadvantage when it comes to requesting the schools to meet your child's special educational needs. While schools are legally required to meet the needs of handicapped students, the process of certifying your child as handicapped requires testing and an individual educational program (IEP), a subject covered in the next chapter.

When Things Have Not Gone Well

Certainly, following the suggestions in this book will help you work smoothly with the school, but occasionally things do not go well. When things are not going well with the school, you need to know what to do. Each state's educational system will have a procedure they would like you to follow. While those procedures may differ from state to state, most of them will follow a similar pattern:

- First, talk to the teacher with whom you are having problems. Explain your concern and listen to his explanation and point of view. Explain your point of view and your child's.
- If the problem is unresolved after talking to the teacher, go to the guidance counselor.
- If the counselor cannot resolve the problem, go to the principal.
- If you are still displeased after talking to the principal, you can file a written complaint with the state board of education.
- You can request state arbitration. Someone from the state board of education will come down and listen to both sides of the complaint.
- You can consider litigation.

Under most circumstances parents will not have to go this far and problems can be resolved at the lower levels. Knowing what your rights are is half the battle. If you know them and the school knows you know them, then there is every likelihood you will never have to use them.

CHAPTER

9

The IEP: What Every Parent Should Know

Under Public Law 94-142, public schools are required to provide handicapped children with an education appropriate to their ability. It is important to know that hyperactivity alone may not qualify a student for special student services. Many of the accompanying problems associated with ADHD, like coordination problems and learning disabilities, do qualify students for these services, and the services are spelled out in an individual educational program (IEP). While IEP forms and procedures may differ from state to state and even from school district to school district within each state, the process remains fairly consistent.

What Is an IEP?

An IEP is a program or a plan for educating your child based on your child's individual educational needs. When properly done, it takes into account your child's disability, his abilities, and his learning style. An IEP should be an action plan, an outline of sorts, spelling out what you and the teachers hope for and how you plan to go about achieving that goal. It could read something like this:

135

John will read at the third-grade level by the end of third grade. He will spend one hour a day in the reading lab with one-on-one instruction and forty minutes Monday, Wednesday, and Friday working at home on the computer with a game call Reading Challenge, using a school-supplied program.

When Is an IEP Necessary?

If teachers suspect your child has a learning disability, emotional problems, or coordination problems, they may take the first step toward an IEP, which is to request testing for the suspected problem. Doctors or psychologists can also request a meeting with the school to draw up an IEP based on information they have and want to share with the school.

How are IEPs Called For?

First, teachers must request the parent's permission to test the child for the suspected problem. In fact, parents get their first hint of an IEP when the school sends home a form requesting testing and evaluation of the child's problems. An IEP usually is proposed after the school has tested and decided that the child has some other type of disability: a speech or hearing problem, an emotional handicap, a physical handicap, or a learning disability. Any or all of these problems are frequently found in hyperactive children and can contribute to hyperactive behavior. If you have a hyperactive child, you should suspect associated difficulties and watch for them as your child develops. A diagnostic team can look at all of these factors, giving the parents and the school the most comprehensive information for an IEP.

While the form should state what areas they would like to look at (i.e., intelligence, emotional adjustment, physical progress, et cetera), parents need to ask what behaviors or classroom incidents prompted the school to call for an IEP. Although teachers and doctors can call for an IEP after testing, parents *cannot* call for an IEP. However, parents *can* request testing if they suspect a problem.

One Oregon teacher was ready to call for an IEP for a child with a suspected speech problem. When she called the parents to tell them she would like to send home a testing request and an IEP form for their daughter, she discovered that the parents, native New Yorkers, had the same speech patterns as the child. The speech "problem" turned out to be nothing more than an unfamiliar accent.

More commonly, IEPs are called for because of growing concern over the child's academic performance or behavioral problems. While schools may make mistakes in diagnosis of hyperactive children and their disabilities, team members, with their highly specialized backgrounds, rarely do. Information provided by a diagnostic team is invaluable to any parent planning an IEP with the school.

When an IEP is called for by the school, parents should view it as an opportunity for their child and begin to prepare both questions and answers for the school. Schools frequently ask parents about their parenting style and discipline methods, as well as their child's developmental history, study habits, and likes (for example, watching TV or playing baseball) and dislikes. Some schools will even ask about your child's schedule and his social life away from school. These are all important questions because they indicate how well your child is adjusting and what areas of his life need some extra attention.

An IEP should be an individualized learning plan that considers your child's unique learning style, handicap, and ability. It is very important that you, as a parent, stress the importance of your child's abilities as well as disabilities. All schools try to help children improve their weak areas, but few are willing to make sure handicapped children continue to excel in the areas where they have real ability. While most schools put forth the best effort possible, they have conflicting interests: teacher schedules, tight budgets, and more work than they can handle. Schools juggle all of these concerns with their concern for your child, and the child does not always come out on top.

Unfortunately, it is true that hyperactivity alone will not qualify children for special student services, although the inability to pay attention is certainly a great handicap to learning. This may change as a result of research done by the National Institute of Mental Health's Dr. Alan Zametkin. His research shows that the brains of hyperactive individuals are physically different. Their brains are considered sluggish and understimulated in certain areas. Just as schools must plan for and allow for the special educational needs of children with cerebral palsy, in the future they will have to allow for the needs of hyperactive children. However, it may be a while before the educational system catches up with the research and what it indicates for the ADHD child.[1]

Once the need for an IEP is established, schools are also required to follow the IEP, provide the special help outlined in it, and do a yearly reevaluation of the child's progress, including a new yearly IEP update reflecting the child's improvements or newly discovered needs. Reevaluations of the IEP are usually done at the beginning of each new school year but may be done at the end of each school year.

What Can You Expect from the School?

Anyone who has ever been through an IEP can tell you what a lonely and intimidating experience it can be. You walk into a teachers' conference room alone to face a large circular table surrounded by five or six people, all in suits, each with a thick file folder with your child's name on it. Suddenly you feel naked, despite your jeans and plaid shirt, and totally inadequate. They, the school officials, tell you how it is and how it is going to be. Sometimes teachers will base criticism of your parenting style and skills on the child's behavior. A comment on parenting may even be included. Everything is written up on a four-copy form called an IEP. While parents may hesitate to sign consent to the IEP or even disagree with the diagnosis or proposed treatment program, usually they feel pressured to sign because this is what the "experts" say is best. If parents still disagree with the diagnosis or the prescribed IEP, often they are informed that it is the only way they will receive help for their child.

Is it any wonder that parents say the IEP is one of the most stressful situations they encounter? It is also one of the most important. Parents can reduce the stress if they are prepared and know what to expect at an IEP; they can also greatly increase their child's chances of success at school.

Who Should Be at Your IEP Meeting?

Different school officials who work with your child are always present at the IEP: the classroom teacher, the principal, the guidance counselor, and the learning center teacher. Sometimes an aide or other teachers will be there. Usually the parents are alone but can bring anyone they would like. Many parents find it much more comfortable if they bring a friend or a member of the diagnostic team. You may feel less intimidated when you have someone there who shares your view of your child. While schools want, and try, to do the very best they can for hyperactive children, problems arise when there is a difference between what the school sees as best and what the parents or diagnostic team sees as best. Here again, the diagnostic team is an important key to the solution to any problems with the schools. When a neutral person chairs or moderates the IEP, it is more likely that everyone will come away from the IEP satisfied. If the parents have paid for a diagnostic team workup, then they may bring a team member to the IEP meeting. If requested, a member of the diagnostic team, usually the child psychologist, will come to the IEP meeting, no matter who paid for the workup. Parents, diagnostic team members, and the school team must all work together as a team for the child to truly benefit.

As we discussed in earlier chapters, the parents are an important part of the process, as are both the diagnostic team and the school team that will ultimately carry out educational plans for your child. You will need to share all of your concerns about your child with the team and discuss any special needs you think your child has. Make sure you discuss all results with the diagnostic team *before* going to the school IEP. It is important for the parents to know what was found by the diagnostic team before it is presented at the school. Team members can answer any questions you may have, and you will have an opportunity for input before the school team becomes involved. This becomes especially important if you are trying to get the school to change their approach to your child or begin a new learning program that they have resisted in the past. If the school and the diagnostic team differ in their diagnosis or corrective treatment, it is important to remember that the team has only one interest: the child. The diagnostic team's plan should be given preference by both the parents and the school. Ideally, both the school and the diagnostic teams will have had adequate parental input before the IEP is drawn up. The IEP will be an opportunity to coordinate an educational program for your child that will increase chances for success in school.

Learning Centers

Corrective or remedial measures proposed in the IEP often include special time spent in a learning center. When a learning disabilities specialist is available for study hall time, this time can be used for limited special help as well. The learning center is usually a self-contained room where a child will get one-on-one attention and intensive help in his weak areas. Under the right conditions this can be a positive opportunity for your child. A good learning center situation should include:

- A qualified teacher with a specialty in learning disabilities.
- A low student:teacher ratio, not to exceed one teacher to five children.
- As much time in the "regular" classroom as possible.
- As little "labeling" as possible.
- Good communication with the home and "regular" class teacher.

Good learning centers should also include some specialized equipment:

- A computer for children who have difficulty writing and for use by ADHD children.
- A hand-held computer speller.
- A tape recorder for children who need to take tests verbally.
- A film-strip machine for children who need visual input to learn.
- A quiet area where a child can work one-on-one with a teacher.
- A learning center room where these activities can go on without distracting other children.
- A set of books with important facts highlighted by the teacher.

Because we now know that hyperactive children can accomplish more on the computer, your child may have to go to the learning center to use one at some time during the day. Learning centers, with their computers, one-on-one teaching, and individualized pace, can give your child a real learning advantage. Eventually your child will have to return to the regular classroom. Successful learning centers help the child overcome his difficulties and return him to the normal classroom as quickly as possible. Their goal is to give the child skills that will allow him to succeed in the regular classroom as well as a special environment.

When your child is back in the regular classroom, you will want to continue to use some practices of the center. One special education teacher offered the following suggestions:

- Have the child sit close to the front of the room where the teacher is.
- Have him do as much as possible on the computer.
- Have two sets of books, one for home and one for school, if possible. (One set should have important information highlighted by the teacher or teacher's aide. ADHD children forget books all the time, and having highlighted (extra set) books at home eliminates lost time, late assignments, and poor grades.)

The Parent as Expert

IEP can also stand for *invaluable experience in parenting.* No one knows your child better than you do, and you need to share with the school what you see your child experiencing. Like parents, teachers see only part of the picture, but you see and know the other parts of your child's life. Teachers know what goes on at school but can only guess what goes on in the child's home. When your child misbehaves every day right before physical education time, the teacher can only wonder if something is wrong at home and the child is misbehaving to gain attention. Parents have to watch and listen, not only to what their child says, but what he is not saying. When your child says, "I hate playground. Mrs. Jones always plays dodgeball, and I am always 'it.' " What he is not saying is: "I have coordination problems, and I run slowly. I would do almost anything, including being punished, to avoid the humiliation of dodgeball." The parents must share their knowledge of the child with both the school and the diagnostic team to give them the full picture of what is happening in the child's life. But parents need to share more than their listening skills; they need to share developmental histories of their child. You need to learn not only to listen, but also to observe as a professional would.

When the Kennedys first took their son, Max, in for a diagnostic team workup, the child psychologist was quite surprised at the file of information they presented. They provided more information than Max's school had, and that information did indeed change how the team saw Max. The Kennedys had started collecting information, observations, medical and scholastic records, and samples of Max's work from the time they first realized Max was different. They made the decision then to become professional advocates for their son.

The Parent as Professional Advocate

From the moment you realize your child is "different" as compared to "normal" children, you need to start behaving like a professional. Start keeping records of the child's health and development; look back and ask yourself when you first noticed particular aspects of his behavior. These records should pick up where your baby book leaves off. Start observing him at home or in his play group and make notes on the observations. (See sample Observation Chart on p. 144.) A good way to do this form is to keep track of the following facts:

You do not have to be formal, but when you bring him home from play group or kindergarten, take a second to jot down some information like: "Johnny sat in circle for twenty seconds, then got up and ran to the swings." If he is not in school yet, take notes on his play activity at home: "Johnny spends hours swinging but does not like cutting paper or drawing with the

Observation Chart

Who:	Johnny	Observer:	Dad
Date:	Dec. 15, 1991	Age:	4 years, 9 months

Time:	Event	Comment
10:45	Johnny plays with a puzzle at the table.	
11:02	Johnny watches the puppets sing.	
11:15	Johnny sits in the circle listening to a story. He picks at his shoe.	He is smiling.
11:16	Johnny leaves group time and runs all the way to the swings.	
11:28	Johnny is ready to go home, but he throws his pictures in the trash. "I do not like them, Mommy. They are not the way I wanted them to be."	His teacher says he has trouble cutting the shapes.

crayons." Keep samples of drawings, date them, and put the child's age on that date on each sample. Be sure to note anything out of the usual, like medical or environmental changes that could affect behavior: "Johnny started a new medication. Johnny has an ear infection. It is allergy season and Johnny has watery eyes and a runny nose." Information and samples of work are very valuable to someone trained in child development or developmental psychology and can help to identify problems that are difficult to diagnose. If a specialist sees a pattern in a number of observations, clues can be found indicating the child's learning style or problem areas.

Whenever your child is tested by the school or the diagnostic team, ask for your own individual copy of test results. Schools can and do lose tests, and it is important for you to keep your own records. Start your own files on your child, even if it is in a cardboard box. Under the Freedom of Information Act, you may see all files on your child that the school has. While they have to let you view these files, they do not have to provide you with a copy. Be prepared to pay for the photocopying of any files you want.

For some parents this information may be coming a little too late. The achievement test was filed in the round file, and the drawings were given to Grandma on her birthday. There is still hope, even for the parent who does not save every scrap of paper. You can make a difference in your child's IEP. If you have not started a file, by all means start one today, but more important, start to prepare today.

How to Have a Better IEP

We started this chapter by telling you what an IEP is like for many parents, but it does not have to be like that, especially if you consider yourself a professional advocate for your child. Professionals follow some basic rules about professional behavior.

First: Go to your IEP Meeting Dressed like a Professional

Professional dress says you are serious about this situation and you demand to be taken seriously. You cannot be intimidated by the other people's wearing suits if you are wearing one, too.

Second: Be Prepared

Bring *your* file folder with information that backs up your feelings or proposed ideas for your child. Be ready to prove your position with facts and evidence in much the same manner the mother in the following example did.

> Despite the fact that Timmy was musically talented, his school was unwilling to put him in the band class because they felt he would not be able to sit still long enough for classes or concerts, but when Timmy's mom presented the school with a note from a local music teacher detailing Timmy's interest and talent in music, the school agreed. Timmy's mother also had a prepared list of questions and was prepared to answer the school's questions. She brought Tim's pediatrician's phone number and a time when the school could reach the pediatrician, who was anxious to be part of the team and to hammer out an IEP that would benefit all areas of Timmy's development.

Some parents know they should make a list of questions but are not sure what they should ask. Some questions you might consider are:

- What made you feel an IEP was necessary?
- How do you think your proposals will improve my child's (speech, learning, social, et cetera) problem?
- What can we do at home to work with these problems?
- Will my child be taken out of the regular classroom?
- For how long each day, each week?
- What subjects will he miss while he is in the learning center?
- Is the school allowing my child to use his special talents?
- What kind of growth or progress can we expect and in what time frame?
- Will my child be labeled?

An IEP can be very beneficial if it provides an opportunity for your child to grow and improve his areas of weakness. For Max, leaving the regular PE class and going to a special physical therapy swimming class accomplished two goals: It relieved the peer pressure to perform athletically at an impossible level, and it helped improve his poor motor skills. Had his IEP required him to miss his math class, an area where he excelled, the gain could have become a total loss.

Third: Take Someone with You

Although there is no scientific evidence to back this up, most mothers are quick to point out that schools listen to fathers better than they do to mothers, so by all means the child's father should attend the IEP if possible. Invite anyone with information on your child who you feel will support your position. Sometimes diagnostic team members are willing to come, and most of the time the child psychologist considers it part of his casework to go to the school with the parents to discuss a proposed course of action.

Fourth: Know Your Legal Rights Before Attending the IEP

The Association for Children with Learning Disabilities is listed in the appendix and, for nothing more than a self-addressed, stamped envelope, will send you a copy of state and federal laws that apply to handicapped children. While the federal laws apply everywhere, state laws will differ, and parents should know all laws that apply to their child before attending the IEP. Read the IEP carefully, and do not sign it unless you agree with the educational goals and activities outlined. If you disagree, put it in writing. Have everyone present sign it and receive a dated copy of it. *You do not have to sign the IEP the day of the meeting;* you can wait, take it home, and discuss it with family members or consult a professional. You have that right.

Fifth: Behave like a Professional

Be firm and assertive but neither hostile nor aggressive. By all means be as polite and cooperative as possible, but do not allow the school to intimidate you or force you to back down on an issue you feel is important. There are two issues you should feel very strongly about: making sure your child receives the extra help he needs and making sure he is not held back because of his disabilities in the areas where he can excel. At one point, the Kennedys' son was held back from a higher math group because he could not complete timed tests due to his motor difficulties. Despite high achievement test scores, he was not placed in the higher math group until his parents became more assertive and brought in members of an outside diagnostic team. No child should be held back because of his disabilities in an area where he is truly capable.

CHAPTER 10

Learning Disability and Hyperactivity: Uncertain Connections

Perhaps all children have problems with school at one time or another. School learning problems may include problems in learning such basic skills as reading, writing, and understanding mathematics. Problems may include difficulty in understanding literature or history. Problems may include motivation or organization in keeping up with required work. Some school learning problems can be explained by lack of ability, lack of encouragement, or poor motivation. For others, school learning problems could be attributed to faulty instruction. But there were always those children who did poorly in school for no clear and understandable reason. There were children who tried, who were supported by family, who went to good schools, who had average—or better—intelligence, but who did not achieve at a level anything like what they, their parents, or their teachers expected. What was the problem?

In 1963 an educational psychologist named Dr. Samuel Kirk gave a keynote address at a conference for educators. He did not focus on what causes learning problems in bright and motivated children. What he proposed was to have schools identify children and provide services for them—children who are learning-disabled—even though the specific cause may not be known. Learning problems probably go back thousands of years, but the term *learning disability,* referring to it as a disorder, goes back only to 1963.

In this chapter we discuss why hyperactive children are clearly at risk for school learning problems. We will present a view of how to determine whether school learning problems of a hyperactive child are due to the hyperactivity itself or are due to a second problem—learning disability. Many parents of children who are evaluated for school learning problems are puzzled about what all the tests are for and what they mean. Through case studies we will try to clarify what the tests are for and how they should be used.

Case Studies

Let us review two children who have serious school learning problems. One of the two children who has a serious learning problem was discovered to have school learning problems associated with hyperactivity. The other child was determined to have a learning disability and showed inattention when he could not function in the classroom.

Hyperactivity plus a School Learning Problem—but Not a Learning Disorder

Paul is a thirteen-year-old boy in a suburban-school eighth grade. He is described as a "bright" youngster but generally receives failing grades. School reports consistently describe him as a youngster who is inattentive, fails to turn in assignments, and talks out of turn. He has gotten into several fights at school during recess. He is often argumentative and talks back to the teacher when corrected. At home he balks at doing chores. On several occasions he has taken money from his parents' purse or wallet. A previous evaluation confirmed a diagnosis of hyperactivity.

In an interview, Paul acknowledges that his behavior is of concern, but he places the blame on others. For example, he admits that his mind wanders or "drifts" in class. But he claims in his defense that when he asks a teacher for clarification he is ignored, as if he should have been on-track. He frequently loses homework or does homework incorrectly and then gets no credit. He recently did a book review and handed it in on time. Part of the purpose of the lesson was for the students to become familiar with the school library. The assignment clearly stated that the book report had to be based on a book checked out of the school library. Paul did not check out a book from the school library. Because he did not follow that rule, he received a failing grade on the assignment. Paul also has a habit of not putting his name on assignments or tests. His teachers automatically give papers a zero if it has no name. Some of his temper outbursts at school involve such times when he believes he was treated unfairly.

Paul received an extensive multidisciplinary or team evaluation at a medical school—based clinic that serves children with handicapping conditions and their families. The focus of this evaluation was school learning and behavior problems. He was administered the Wechsler Intelligence Scale for Children—III (WISC—III).

The Wechsler Intelligence Scale for Children—III

The WISC—III consists of a verbal scale of the test, which assesses a child's ability to understand the meaning of words, to solve problems and express answers orally, to solve arithmetic problems mentally and to recall information learned in the past, and to remember series of numbers presented during the testing session. A second section of the test, the performance scales, evaluates a child's ability to solve problems when words (language) are not the main issue. The scales evaluate a child's ability to look at a design and construct it with blocks, to solve novel puzzles, to copy a series of symbols in which speed and quick learning of novel symbols are important, and to look at a series of pictures and recognize missing details.

During the assessment Paul showed a high activity level. He

was active and frequently rocked his chair back and forth. He was fidgety and quite talkative, and it was necessary to redirect him several times during the test. The results, however, indicated he was functioning within the average range of intelligence, with a verbal IQ score of 98, a performance IQ score of 102, and a full scale IQ score of 100. The average range of IQ scores on the WISC—III is 85 to 115. About 66 percent of children in the United States score in the normal range. Paul showed relative weakness on four of the subtests, *information, arithmetic, digit span, and coding.* Weakness on those subtests is consistent with problems maintaining sustained attention.

Paul was also administered portions of the Woodcock-Johnson Psycho-Educational Battery pertaining to reading, math, written language, and science achievement. The test results showed that his achievement level was at or above his grade level in reading, math, written language, and science.

Behavior Rating Scales

As part of the information obtained for the evaluation, each of Paul's teachers completed the Conners form for teachers. The teacher form consists of twenty-eight items, and it measures behavior problems and hyperactivity. Each of the teachers who taught Paul in academic-oriented classes rated Paul in a way consistent with hyperactivity. He received high scores on such items as excitable, impulsive, restless, always "on the go," distractibility, or attention-span problems. He was also noted to disturb other children and to have temper outbursts and unpredictable behavior.

Each parent also filled out the Connors parent questionnaire, and the parents also rated Paul in a way that was consistent with ADHD.

Paul was determined *not* to have a learning disability. He did have school learning problems and was failing at his grade placement. His achievement—what he actually had learned—was at grade level and consistent with his intellectual skills. His poor performance at school can be explained by ADHD. He is in-attentive, often off-track, and frankly careless with assignments.

Diagnostic Statement Regarding Paul

PROBLEM: ADHD

NOTE: Although he has maintained his standing relative to his classmates in basic academic skills, his school performance is negatively affected by or-ganizational problems. School and home-based plans are designed to maintain standards for be-havior and learning while helping him to com-pensate for attentional problems.

Educational Plan for Paul

Treatment for Paul, as is true for most children with hyperac-tivity, required a multimodal approach. The treatment plan was constructed by a treatment team that consisted of his parents, his teachers, his physician, and a mental health professional (clinical psychologist). The plan consisted of both a school-based management program and a home-based behavior management program. Without a well thought out plan Paul would be at near certain risk to experience continued school failure, increased conflict with his family, and rejection by peers. This pattern could lead to serious emotional problems.

School-Based Recommendations on Testing and an IEP Meeting

Paul had a pattern of not handling changes well. He was often disruptive during recess, during transition from one class to another, or when there were changes in schedule and during field trips. The rules for behavior during these times would be reviewed with Paul and his behavior monitored.

There were several recommendations that were implemented

for giving instructions to Paul. First, the teachers made it clear to Paul that if he needed assistance he would be helped and not just reminded that he should have paid attention. This was to encourage Paul to feel comfortable asking for assistance.

Second, the teachers would make sure that Paul understood instructions before doing assignments. There were several things that teachers could do to assure this, including having Paul repeat instructions before starting a task. This would reduce the number of times that Paul worked on assignments but received failing grades because he missed the point of the assignment.

Third, Paul was required to have a daily assignment book. Since Paul has good writing skills, it was his responsibility to write down assignments each day. The assignment book was reviewed for accuracy by the teachers. When assignments were completed the book would be signed by parents and teachers. The parents were encouraged to comment on or discuss with the teachers any questions that arose about assignments or schoolwork.

Fourth, to encourage active participation in the learning process, Paul was given opportunities to lead discussions in areas where he had demonstrated competence in small teacher-monitored student groups.

Accommodations or Departures from Established School Policy

The school had a general policy that by the eighth grade assignments and school work had to be in on time. Late work was not accepted. The rule was designed to teach responsibility and also to keep children focused on current school lessons so as not to be distracted by a large number of incomplete assignments. Paul, however, did not have the maturity, the work habits, or the organizational skills to cope with what was ordinarily a good rule. For Paul, his teachers agreed on a plan to accept late assignments and to deduct only a modest amount (10 percent) for papers or assignments that were turned in late. This maintained the expectation that schoolwork was to be done on time. He would also receive only a modest deduction (10 percent of earned grade) if he failed to place his name on an assignment. This plan meant a change in an established rule; for Paul late work would be accepted.

Of interest is that both the school and the parents agreed to the plan, but initially Paul did not. At first he was adamant that he did not want to be treated differently than other children. His reaction was not unusual. Many hyperactive children hate being singled out. A comment such as "Did you take your medication?" in front of classmates can be devastating to a child. It is important to acknowledge and recognize a student's reaction to any change from normal or typical procedure and to discuss with the student the reasons why a change is being considered. Paul did not want the privilege of getting an extra chance to hand in work after a deadline. He was confronted firmly but without anger about his behavior of not doing the work in a timely manner and often not doing important parts of assignments. The rule of no late work being accepted was changed to give him credit for what he could learn and accomplish. The accommodation was made not to reduce expectations, but to keep expectations at a level appropriate for the child.

At home there were changes in chores and amount of time spent on homework. It is important that children have a chance to discuss changes that are about to take place. It is also important that such topics as chores and homework be presented as tasks relevant for the child.

School Learning Problems: Learning Disability and Secondary Inattention

Brian, another thirteen-year-old boy, was referred to a learning disorders clinic by his pediatrician. As a young child Brian seemed to develop normally, except that he showed some delay in speech. He had trouble pronouncing words. This has been resolved and his speech is now understandable. Brian showed academic difficulties as early as kindergarten. He was retained for a second year in first grade. He was diagnosed as having a learning disability while in the second grade. He recently completed sixth grade, where he received special services for reading, language, spelling, and math.

Outside of school, Brian does better. He is very good at fixing things. He enjoys outdoor activities, especially boating and fishing.

Test of Intellectual Functioning

As part of the evaluation, Brian was administered the WISC—III. He was cooperative and attentive and gave good effort during the evaluation. Brian's test performance shows definite patterns of strengths and weaknesses in his intellectual functioning, against a background of an overall IQ score that was within normal limits. He achieved a verbal IQ score of 94, a performance IQ score of 103, and a full scale IQ score of 99.

Brian showed great difficulty on three subtests: arithmetic, digit span, and coding. This suggests he has deficits in concentration, attention, and short-term memory. He was able to repeat only three digits (numbers) forward on each of two tries and four digits forward inconsistently. He was able to repeat only two digits backward consistently and was inconsistent when the item called for him to repeat three digits backward. This ability to recall and repeat digits is about at the level of a six-year-old child. Brian had comparable difficulty solving simple arithmetic problems in which he had to remember the question. On the coding subtest he was to look at a series of numbers, each with a special mark below it. For the test itself, he was supposed to put in the marks that were to go below the numbers that appeared on his answer sheet. Brian had great difficulty with this test. It was clear that as the testing proceeded he did not remember any of the marks or symbols as they appeared again on the test. Each trial (or each mark) was like a first experience for him. This task for Brian was laborious and difficult.

On the other hand, Brian did well on tasks such as picture completion, picture arrangement, block design, and object assembly subtests. He was able to show an organized approach to the task. His performance on these subtests was not affected by his difficulty in auditory processing and in memory. Other strengths include an overall good vocabulary.

Assessment of Academic Achievement

READING AND WRITING

As part of the evaluation, Brian's reading skills were assessed to help plan an appropriate instructional program for him. This portion of the assessment consisted of a record review, an interview with Brian's teacher and resource room teacher, a behavior observation in the classroom, an interview with his mother, an individualized assessment using curriculum-based reading materials currently being used with Brian, and the decoding subsections of the Woodcock Reading Mastery Test.

Curriculum-Based Reading Assessments

Brian was asked to read out loud the letters of the alphabet. This was part of a series of probes to assess his decoding skills. Brian was able to correctly read twenty-two of twenty-six letters of the alphabet. His errors consisted of saying "d" for "b," "m" for "w," and vice versa. He was then asked to pronounce common letter combinations that together make a single sound (phonemes). He had great difficulty with this part of the test. He read slowly, hesitantly, and inaccurately. When whole words were presented he again responded slowly with a high error rate. His errors included changing the ending of words: *face* for *fact*, *there* for *then*; substituting the letter *b* for *d*, *bad* for *dad*, *bud* for *dude*; and substituting one vowel sound for another, *bike* for *bake*, *seat* for *set*. It was clear that he had not mastered the decoding necessary for reading.

Reading Comprehension Skills Assessment: Written Retell

Brian was presented with a short story from one of his current reading books. The story that Brian read was about the four seasons of the year and how a person adapts to weather changes. Brian spent five minutes reading the story and then was to write down everything he remembered about the story.

His written response after reading the story consisted of one five-word sentence.

Wn bak as dork set.

When asked about what he wrote, he said, "My bike has a broken seat." He was then asked to retell any other part of what he read. He responded, "I don't remember." Like many learning-disabled children with a severe deficit in reading skills, Brian found his most severe problem was that he got so little information from what he read.

In all, Brian's reading skill level is at the first-grade level.

Comprehension of Orally Presented Material

Brian was read stories that were at the level of an eighth-grade student. This time he was to listen and be prepared to answer questions about what he heard. It was already established that Brian had difficulty with short-term memory for orally presented material. For this portion of the testing Brian was told he could ask questions about what was read to him or even have the entire passage repeated. This was done to determine if Brian could grasp the material if the pacing of the information was adjusted for him. Brian showed good comprehension of the stories and was able to paraphrase or restate the main points of what was read to him. He also showed evidence of a good vocabulary, which is consistent with the results of the intelligence test.

FORMAL ASSESSMENT OF BRIAN'S MATH SKILLS

Standardized assessment of Brian's math concepts and skills showed that he was at the first-to-second-grade level, far below his grade placement. Math presents a triple jeopardy for Brian:

1. He cannot read written math.
2. He has a poor memory for information presented orally.
3. He has conceptual skills in mathematics far below his grade level.

INFORMAL ASSESSMENT OF MATH CONCEPTS

It is possible to use an interview to probe about a person's understanding of math in everyday use. Brian happened to have with him a set of baseball cards. The cards became a focus during a brief interview that indirectly provided a way of evaluating his ability to count, to subtract, and to understand percentages.

A portion of the interview went as follows:

PSYCHOLOGIST: You have mentioned that you like outdoor activities. Are there any sports or activities that you especially like?
BRIAN: I like to play baseball.
PSYCHOLOGIST: What positions have you played?
BRIAN: I have played first base, outfield, and I have been a pitcher.

Brian expresses enthusiasm while talking about baseball.

PSYCHOLOGIST: Do you consider yourself a good hitter?
BRIAN: Yes!

Brian reaches into his jacket pocket and carefully pulls out an envelope containing about twelve baseball cards.

PSYCHOLOGIST: Oh, can I see your cards?

BRIAN: Sure.

PSYCHOLOGIST: Which is your favorite?

BRIAN: The one about Jose Canseco.

PSYCHOLOGIST: Do you remember what his lifetime batting average is?

BRIAN: No, I don't know.

PSYCHOLOGIST: Do you know what your own batting average is?

BRIAN: No, not really.

PSYCHOLOGIST: Let's suppose that in a game you went to bat four times and you got a double, a single, and also struck out one time and then flied out to center. Do you know what your batting average would be for that game?

BRIAN: I really don't know.

PSYCHOLOGIST: Did you buy these cards?

BRIAN: Yes, I did; they cost $1.20.

PSYCHOLOGIST: If you gave the clerk two one-dollar bills, how much change would you get back?

BRIAN: I don't know.

PSYCHOLOGIST: Take your time; think about it.

The psychologist repeats the question. Brian answers hesitantly.

BRIAN: Twenty cents?

PSYCHOLOGIST: How many baseball cards do you have in this packet?

Brian counts them and correctly states: Twelve!

Comment about the Interview

Information from this interview helped the parents understand that Brian's delayed math skills were making it hard for Brian to understand and communicate about his world.

Parent Conference

After the extensive evaluations, both parents were present to hear the results of the evaluation. Later there would be an individualized educational planning meeting to develop an IEP.

In the parent conference the parents reviewed their concerns and their questions about Brian and his severe problems with academic work. The parents knew that Brian was struggling at school and that he had been having difficulties with schoolwork since kindergarten. They were concerned about both the boy's education and the increased frustration he experienced.

The results of the evaluation were reviewed with the parents, including the fact that Brian has overall normal intelligence, but that he showed problems with short-term memory. His academic skill levels were reviewed, and it was stressed that his reading level was so low that he had little comprehension of any information that was provided in written form. He was also delayed in math skills, which would be compounded if he had to read a math question. Since there was a severe gap between his intelligence level and his reading, writing, and math skills, this qualified him as eligible for specialized services at school.

Diagnostic Statement Regarding Brian

PROBLEM: Learning Disabilities, Reading (Dyslexia), and Math Problems

NOTE: This boy has overall normal intelligence. There is a severe gap between his intelligence level, his reading and writing skills, and his math skills. He is eligible for specialized services at school.

What is Meant by Learning Disability—How Is It Defined?

Many educators and psychologists actually read to a parent a definition of a learning disability to help the parent understand the disorder and the reasons why his child needs special assistance in school. The following definition was published in 1968, but still holds true today.

> Children with special learning disabilities exhibit a disorder in one or more of the basic psychological processes involved in understanding or in using spoken or written language. These may be manifested in disorders of listening, thinking, talking, reading, writing, spelling or arithmetic. They include conditions which have been referred to as perceptual handicaps, brain injury, minimal brain dysfunction, dyslexia, developmental aphasia, etc. They do not include learning problems which are due primarily to visual, hearing or motor handicaps, mental retardation, emotional disturbance or environmental disadvantage. (U.S. Office of Education, 1968, p.34).

Note that the definition is broad and is meant to include children who, for one or more reasons, have difficulty with academic work in spite of overall normal intelligence and opportunity. The definition excludes children who may have difficulty with schoolwork for reasons that already make them eligible for special services, such as hearing problems or mental retardation.

What Causes a Learning Disability?

There are large numbers of medical conditions that place children at risk for learning disability. Some involve neurological problems such as cerebral palsy, spina bifida, and epilepsy. Children who are known to have Fetal Alcohol Syndrome are at risk for developmental delay, and some will be learning-disabled. Also, if a child suffers a serious head trauma in an accident *and* shows problems with attention, speech, and language impairment or motor coordination, the child may develop a learning disability secondary to, or associated with, the head trauma. None of these links to learning disability are clearcut. Each case must be assessed individually. Some children with established neurological problems will not have symptoms of a learning disability. In most cases of learning disability an established neurological disorder, independent of the learning disability, is not present.

In most cases, the specific cause of the learning disability is not known and the problem, unfortunately, cannot be detected until it develops. In Brian's case there are no obvious medical factors that explain it. However, we do know that Brian had early problems with language development. In his case that may be the link to his learning disability.

What is the Best Treatment Plan for Brian?

There is no single treatment plan for children with a learning disability. The term IEP or individualized education plan, is meant to convey the idea that a child with a learning disability can learn, but requires a plan that is designed for the child. There is no blueprint that can be used for *all* children with a learning disability.

In Brian's case he will clearly need specialized assistance in reading and math and, in my opinion, he should take exams that deal with content or information orally. We recommend that prior to the IEP meeting, you review his records as well as the various reports—including the psychological evaluation. This should help you as you participate in the IEP meeting.

PLAN: Brian does have a good vocabulary, and he is able to attend to and comprehend much information that is presented orally. He should be encouraged to participate in mainstream classes to the extent that much of the material is presented orally and in which supplementary materials are available on tapes. For those

classes he should not take written tests when his skill
levels are only at the first-grade level. Exams should
be given orally, with Brian permitted to express his
answers verbally.

THE USE OF AUDIOTAPES FOR NONREADERS

The use of audiotapes by learning-disabled students who are
either nonreaders or severly impaired readers has potential problems. It is inefficient to have to listen to whole sections of a
class lecture again and again or to listen to tape-recorded books
in their entirety over and over again. Brian was taught to use a
tape recorder to take notes. He could use it as if it were a note
pad. He learned to paraphrase and to restate main points con-
cisely. This also prepared him for taking exams. Brian would
do his note taking in a resource room or study room after a
class session. This eliminated the possibility that his dictation
would disturb other students.

READING INSTRUCTIONS FOR LEARNING-DISABLED
STUDENTS

CHOICES IN STRATEGIES: PHONICS VERSUS A WHOLE
LANGUAGE OR HOLISTIC APPROACH

Parents of learning-disabled students are usually confronted with
educational plans for their children without a background to
evaluate them. There are two major and very different approaches to teaching reading. One is known as a phonics approach; the other is referred to as a holistic or whole language
approach. For comparison purposes we will present a brief background on each approach and then a plan as they might apply
to Brian. We do not feel that one approach is the best for all
children with a learning disability. We encourage parents to be
informed and to ask questions.

Phonics Approach

A phonics approach to teaching reading can be compared to a building block approach. It assumes that a child learns to read through knowing particular skills. In the phonics approach a child is taught isolated skills of recognizing sounds and letters. It does involve much repetition, and often a child does not move on to new material until specific skills are mastered. Comprehension of written material is assumed to come naturally when the child is able to correctly decode (read) the written material. If Brian were to be enrolled in a phonics-based program, his IEP might read as follows:

Regarding reading, Brian should be taught a phonetics-based decoding strategy. He should have large numbers of opportunities to respond with immediate and consistent feedback. Brian should demonstrate mastery of material before attempting new information. Brian should spend about an hour a day doing homework. Of that time, about fifteen minutes should be spent reviewing previously learned reading materials. In order to avoid developing new error patterns, he should not be presented with new reading material until he demonstrates that past material is learned.

The remainder of the home study time should be spent listening to tapes of books that cover materials being studied at school. His parents should look to verbal (oral) answers regarding questions and homework assignments rather than written responses.

Whole Language or Holistic Approach

Whereas a phonics approach stresses the learning of specific skills in order to read, the whole language or holistic approach stresses reading for meaning, with the idea that specific skills are learned naturally through reading for meaning. A whole language approach stresses reading and writing as a natural form of communication, like talking and listening. It stresses context and not words in isolation. In a whole language approach a child may be encouraged to tell a story. The teacher would write the story and have the child read it. The child could then be asked questions about the words. The details of reading (decoding) are learned as the child reads without the seemingly endless repetition that may take place in a phonics-based approach. Many children learn to read naturally in homes in which parents read and tell stories to children. The child sees reading and writing as important parts of his life and not activities that are unnecessarily structured and drilled. Teachers who follow the holistic approach recognize that children are better at constructing knowledge from their experiences then teachers are at trying to break learning into small, manageable pieces.

A whole language or holistic approach for Brian might read as follows:

> Brian should be given opportunities to read and write for purposes that are important and meaningful for him. For example, he may be encouraged to tell a story while his reading teacher writes it down. He could then be encouraged to "read" his story and ask questions about it. Notes that Brian tapes in paraphrased form could be transcribed as reading exercises for Brian. He should be encouraged to use context to get at the meaning of the communication. The teacher will need to address how Brian attempts to get meaning from the passages and not just focus on word attack skills. Writing for Brian should also flow from what he is learning. He should be encouraged to talk out loud or say what he plans to write and then put the words on paper. Records of his writing should be dated and kept to evaluate progress. The teacher will need to observe for recurring error patterns and provide specific feedback. Brian should be encouraged to revise his writing by the teacher emphasizing that most good writers in fact write by revising earlier drafts.

MATH INSTRUCTION FOR BRIAN

There is much that can be done at home and at school to provide Brian with opportunities to use math in a functional way. For example, he could regularly be involved with establishing a personal budget and participate in shopping and keeping track of prices and costs. He can be drawn into measuring objects by length and weight and applying numbers and concepts as ways for him to understand more about his world and to communicate about them. He should be encouraged to measure his fish and to keep track of baseball statistics, including learning how to compute batting averages. Currently, Brian tends to guess when he is uncertain, and his estimates are often far off the mark. He may need help in developing strategies to make reasoned approximations rather than "pull numbers out of a hat." Until his reading improves, he will still need reliance on math problems presented orally. He should be encouraged to ask questions if he fails to remember any or all of the math problems. As he develops basic math concepts, it will then be possible to introduce more advanced concepts.

Hyperactivity Versus Learning Disabilities: Uncertain Connections

The two boys who represent examples for this chapter were similar in that they both had school learning problems. But they did so for different reasons.

Paul was hyperactive but did not have a learning disability. ADHD, by itself, does not seem to affect the brain's ability to learn. Paul was at grade level in basic academic skills. Paul did not require specialized services at school. But he did need some accommodation at school so that he would have more time to redo schoolwork when he misunderstood assignments, lost them, or didn't do them. This accommodation was made to maintain appropriate expectations for school achievement and performance. He also was involved in a behavior modification program at home to set behavioral objectives and rewards for chores and homework completion. He also was placed on treatment with medication, which helped him pay attention in school and reduced his impulsivity.

Brian, in contrast, had a learning disability. He did need specialized services at school. His resource room teacher had special training to work with children with learning disabilities. Brian needed and received accommodation in the form of taped texts, and he had a reader assigned to him at times during the week. Tests were modified so that he could give answers orally and not in writing. This was done so he could be evaluated on what he had learned, rather than having him display his disability every time he had to take a test. He did continue to receive instruction in reading, but it was individualized and the pacing was adjusted to his progress. The reading material was adjusted to age-appropriate interest levels. Brian did show lapses of attention in school, but they were not signs of ADHD. For him, when he was hopelessly unable to understand information when given in written form he lost interest and appeared inattentive.

We introduce the words *uncertain connections* in discussing ADHD and learning disabilities very deliberately. It is correct that children with ADHD as well as children with learning disabilities have difficulty learning and performing in school. In some cases—as represented by Paul and Brian—their difficulties stem from very different reasons. However, children with ADHD are at greater risk than other children of having a learning disability. In those cases both disorders ought to be diagnosed and countered with appropriate treatment plans. Children with a learning disability may be inattentive, restless, and frustrated in school situations where they cannot function. If their inattention is restricted to those situations, then they should not be diagnosed as having ADHD. The uncertainty can be resolved by careful diagnosis.

Connections Between Learning Disability and Emotional/Behavioral Problems

Brian happened to be a well-behaved boy. At times he would become moody, and occasionally he complained of stomachaches. Some children with learning disabilities develop serious emotional, behavioral, and family problems. When this occurs it may be due to the very high frustration these children encounter in such an important area of their lives as schoolwork.

A neurological problem that contributes to school learning problems in children with learning disability may also contribute to problems in social behavior and in poor anger control.

Learning disabilities in a minority of cases can predispose an individual to conduct-disorder problems. Dr. Leif Terdal, a psychologist, recalls receiving referrals from a school such as: "We want an assessment of his personality and emotional adjustment. This boy is dangerous and we want to know how to control him. We do not want an IQ test or educational tests." It is not uncommon when the multidisciplinary team evaluates such children to find a previously undetected severe learning disability. The child's poor school performance is blamed on incorrigible behavior. However, the cause-effect relationship may be just the opposite. The very disturbed and aggressive behavior shown by some children with a learning disability may be caused by the same neurological problem that caused the learning disability, plus unrelenting frustrations due to continuing experiences of failure.

ADHD Teens

Adolescence and Early Adulthood

For all children, normal or hyperactive, adolescence is a difficult time of life. Sometime in junior high all children experience rapid growth and hormonal changes as prepubescence rapidly turns into adolescence. *This is a time of great social awareness for all children,* as they try to find their niche in the school's social scene. It is a time when emotions run high and feelings are tender. Some of the preadolescent behavioral changes parents see in average children make them wonder if their child is hyperactive. With the exception of cases in which a child suffers minimal brain damage caused by a sudden accident, hyperactivity rarely, if ever, begins in adolescence.

The truly hyperactive child will experience all of the normal changes associated with puberty. While hyperactive children experience the same things "normal" children do, they are also at greater risk during these years and require careful parenting. Unfortunately, this difficult period for parents comes at a time when the parents of ADHD children are already worn out from years of heavy-duty parenting. Many parents are tempted to give up and say, "I've already done all I can do. If he hasn't learned by now, he never will."

Hang in there. Adolescence is a time when careful planning and diligent parenting will pay off. If you have used positive discipline and your child has a positive self-concept, you are already one step ahead of the game.

While ADHD children may have a little more difficulty and

require a little more help than some adolescents, they do make it through. Some of the strategies covered in this book will help you and your child make it through a little easier. In this chapter we are going to look at some of the trouble spots for ADHD teens. The two areas teens are most concerned about are their social life and school. However, parents look beyond their child's teen years to his future; two areas that concern parents are preparing the child to live independently and to hold onto a job. We are going to talk about all four of these areas and share some of the things that can be done to help your child succeed in each area.

Social Life

Because many hyperactive children have difficulty succeeding in school, the peer group can become even more important to them. Because of their low self-esteem, hyperactive children are easy targets for gangs and drug abuse problems. You will want to pay close attention to the friendships your child forms. It is important to get your child involved in a social group as early as possible in junior high. Band, swim team, and scouts are all excellent group activities. Of course, you will want to have him choose a group he is interested in and where he has some skill.

Building Teen Friendships

While social skills have always been important for ADHD children, they become even more important in junior high and high school. All children want friends. When ADHD children cannot fit into the more popular groups because of their poor social skills, they start to look for any group that will accept them. Sometimes they have trouble making friends because they do not pick up on social cues.

You may need to teach them to look out for the social cues

they are not picking up. The Kennedys noticed that their son, Max, did not respond when classmates passed him in the hall and said "Hello." Max was so used to trying to filter out noise, he just ignored friends' voices in the noisy hall as "more noise."

"Max," his parents said, "when people say hello to you, they're showing you they care about you and how you're feeling today. You need to show them you care about them, too, and respond by saying, 'Hi. How are you?'" What seems obvious to all of us was not obvious to Max. After Max's parents pointed out the social cue, he no longer ignored it. Because his guidance counselor was with him at school and his parents were not, the counselor made a point of indicating social cues over the years, and it was a big help to Max. Each time it changed Max's behavior and helped him grow socially.

Another way to build friendships is to start with the teenager's interests. After-school clubs are a good place to start. If your child likes computers, the computer club will offer some good options. There are many sports clubs that place little or no emphasis on competition, but only on enjoyment of the game, like golf club or chess club. In these clubs your child can meet people and take part in group activities.

Unfortunately, even in high school, you will probably have to be the one to have your child's friends over. That is all right; at least you know where they are and what they are doing. Having a group of high-schoolers over requires as much planning as having kindergarteners over. Rent movies and center the evening around a theme or activity, like horseback riding or a pizza party followed by an Italian movie. Have games on hand that teens like, like Pictionary or Trivial Pursuit. If you have them over, at least it is your house and you get to make the rules, and there must be rules.

Dating

Parents of both boys and girls worry about their impulsive child dating. You will find it helpful to use some of the same principles we have talked about earlier as you try to have your child "think" before he acts or reacts. Because they do not pick up on social cues, ADHD children are higher risk for unplanned pregnancy and ADHD boys are at higher risk of forcing girls into something they do not want to do. Here are some suggestions to reduce the risks.

EXPLAIN TO YOUR SON

Nick, when a girl says no, you have to stop, no matter how difficult that may be. You can't force girls to do something they do not want to do. That is rape. That means even if they change their mind and they wanted to before, you have to stop.

EXPLAIN TO YOUR DAUGHTER

Polly, I know you consider yourself a grown-up, and I know your friends are all dating. Grown-ups follow the rules, and there are some rules for dating.

SET RULES

- "You may date if you go out with a group of people." (There is safety in numbers.)
- "Dad and I don't go anywhere without telling you where we are going, and we expect the same courtesy. We need to know where you are and whom you're with." (Always know where they are and whom they are with.)
- "You may have your friend over to our house *when we are home.*"
- "Don't lead boys on. Sometimes boys get the wrong message, so make sure you tell them clearly that you don't want to have sex."
- Let your son know that girls may flirt while being friendly and they may feel they are being lead on, but that doesn't mean the girls want to have sex.
- While your children will get sex education in school, you

are the best person to talk to them about your values. Have a frank discussion with your son or daughter and tell him or her that sex is a grown-up act requiring grown-up responsibilities. Do not be afraid to tell your child that you do not want him or her to have sex until he or she is a mature adult. Tell your child that when he or she is an adult, he or she will need to take the adult responsibility of producing a pregnancy only when it is wanted and loved.

- Be sure to tell your child about AIDS and other sexually transmitted diseases. Be sure they understand that some of them are deadly, and others (herpes) last forever.
- Make sure they understand what you are talking about.

Academic Success

School is another area of great concern during the teen years. Working with school members of your team can be even more important in the high school years than it was when the child was younger. Producing a coordinated effort can pay off if your child goes through high school and his teen years with a positive self-concept as well as some measure of academic and social success. Helping your child succeed in school is one of the best things you can do to prepare him for the future. A big part of academic success is homework.

Homework

When Dr. Terdal interviews a child about homework he does so with the idea in mind of reviewing what the child normally does and considering that against what might be expected for other children of that age. He stresses that he needs to get a sense of what actually happens and not exaggerated claims. He also explains to the child that he will need to review schoolwork and homework assignments turned in with both parents and his teachers. Most children then give a report that is pretty close to information independently provided by parents and teachers. The following excerpt of an interview with Mike occurred in the middle of an interview, after rapport was established and the issue of problems at school were reviewed with him.

TERDAL: Mike, how much homework do you do?
MIKE: It depends.
TERDAL: It depends on what?
MIKE: Sometimes 1 don't get any homework, and some-
          times I forget to bring it home. Sometimes the
          homework I get I can do in two minutes.
TERDAL: Two minutes!
MIKE: Two minutes.
TERDAL: Mike, you and I know that you have ability. Your
          reading skills and math skills are pretty good. I
          want you to imagine that you have good athletic
          skills. Imagine that you can run fast, that you can
          throw a ball accurately, and that you can jump. I
          want you to imagine that you are about to meet a
          track coach at your school. You tell him that you
          want to try out for his team and that you want to
          run the 200-meter and 400-meter races. Tell the
          coach that you want to be a star athlete but that
          you want to do it on *two minutes'* practice a day.
          You will give the effort two minutes a day.

Mike knew such a time commitment for a sport would be absurd. At age thirteen, Mike should spend a full hour to an hour and a half a day at homework. If he has no assigned work, he should send an hour reading, writing, or reviewing math work. This time should increase each year through high school.

HOMEWORK PROBLEMS: "LET'S GET ON WITH IT"

It is critical when instituting a strictly monitored homework plan that the results be positive for the student. The most common problem for hyperactive children is the attitude of "let's get on with it." A parent must be alert to this and must deal with it carefully. In Mike's case he did agree to increase time spent on homework. But there were problems. His mother customarily reviewed his math homework. She often noticed several errors, including errors indicating that Mike had not carefully read the instructions. His answers were not related to the questions. When she confronted Mike (which she should do) about the errors, Mike usually replied, "Mom, I have so much homework to do that I can't possibly recheck any answers. I must get on with it." This pattern must be stopped. A child will not benefit from careless and superficial efforts. Teachers understand how serious and self-defeating the repetition of poor work habits can be for students. Quality is more important than amount of effort or quantity. If you honestly believe that your child has too much homework to do it well, say so. If you believe that your child does not have enough homework, say so. Let's do it right—let's not just "get on with it."

With the support of his parents and his teachers—and with increased effort by Mike—he earned an eighth-grade graduation and was ready to continue on. It was not an easy year for everyone involved. There were lapses, but Mike *earned* passing grades.

Preparation for Adult Life

Setting Goals

One of the first things you need to do is set realistic goals *with* your hyperactive child. It is good to want the best for your child, but remember, your "wants" have to be defined by reality. Hyperactivity is a disability. While hyperactive children cannot be cured, they can do better, and they can work on skills that will help them to become happy, self-supporting, and independent adults.

As your child grows older, you will want to make sure that he develops the skills needed to live independently. Some high schools offer classes called Living on Your Own or the like. Even if your local high school has an independence course like this, you will want to reinforce it with frequent practice of those skills. Teens need to know how to shop for their own clothes, how to shop for, prepare, and serve meals, how to pay bills, and how to keep their surroundings clean.

All children pick up some of these skills along the way as they do chores around the house, but some skills must be taught. By the time a child is in junior high, he should begin to shop for and prepare one meal a week. You can begin the process when the child is much younger by asking him to help you plan dinner one night a week. Everyone in the family can choose (and plan) one dinner a week. As they grow older, they can be phased into shopping and preparing and cleaning up after a dinner once a week.

As teens mature, parents can expect them to do more chores and to accept responsibilities like homework. It is important that children have a chance to discuss changes in chores and expectations that are about to take place. Typically, the hyperactive adolescent is not "motivated" to do chores or to in any way learn the skills needed to take care of himself, but neither are many other teens. However, this area is so important that Dr. Terdal routinely covers it with his preadolescent and adolescent ADHD clients. Sometimes he approaches it through a child interview, like the following one he did with another child, David.

David's Chore Interview

When Dr. Terdal reviews chores with a child who has ADHD, he reviews the responsibilities the child has that prepare the child for future roles. Young adults, eighteen years and older, should be able to plan and prepare meals, maintain a house or apartment, and live within a budget. Dr. Terdal reviews these points with the child and stresses that he needs to know usual and typical behavior. He reviews these issues in terms of the child's age and ability. He lets the child know that he will get independent information from the parents. Surprisingly, a child's report is often very close to that of a parent's.

This is how portions of the interview went with David:

TERDAL: What chores do you have that are understood in your family as your responsibility?

DAVID: I am supposed to take out the garbage on Tuesday mornings, and I am supposed to keep my room clean.

TERDAL: You are thirteen years old. At this age you should be able to handle meal preparation for your family. This means planning for a meal, preparing it, serving it, and cleaning up afterward. The whole sequence. Do you do that?

DAVID: No, I never have.

TERDAL: Okay. We will have to work on that. When you are eighteen you will be an adult. You will need to be responsible for house maintenance. This means all the work that might take place each week: vacuum cleaning, mopping floors, cleaning the kitchen and the bathroom, washing and drying clothing, and working on the yard. Do you take a turn at the whole job?

DAVID: No! I never have done any of all of that.

TERDAL: Okay, let me write that down. We will come back to that. Who buys your clothes?

DAVID: My mother does.

TERDAL: David, let's get this straight. You are thirteen years old. In time you will have to plan a budget. This means understanding how much it costs to keep you fed, clothed, and equipped with school supplies.

We will review this again. I want you to begin
thinking about the money that your family spends
for your care. You should begin to assume responsibility to work within a budget. I don't mean that
you should earn your keep. That is your parents'
responsibility. But you should understand the costs
and be able to understand how to budget.

After reviewing the child's behavior in relation to chores that
prepare him for life tasks, Dr. Terdal asks the child what additional chores he will commit to. If the child counters with a
statement like, "I will take out the garbage and clean my room"
(at thirteen), the psychologist says, "That won't do it. We need
to go beyond the garbage can." Most children, even ADHD
children, understand that, and a commitment to plan is a first
step.

Follow-up Note on Chores

David, our thirteen-year-old, agreed that he would plan, prepare, and serve a meal for the family and do the cleanup after
the meal one evening a week. He chose Sunday night to be his
"turn." He loved bouillabaisse, a fish soup that his mother
would make with a tomato-base sauce, scallops, steamer clams,
spices, and fish. It was served in a bowl with rice.

On the first Sunday, David strutted out to the kitchen. He
announced, "I'm going to serve bouillabaisse."

His mother looked at him in amazement: *Does he have the
ingredients?* she thought.

He opened the pantry door and blurted, "Mom, where do
you have the cans of bouillabaisse?"

David, at the age of thirteen years, did not know that when
his mother served bouillabaisse she made it from scratch. His
mother did not live in a turn-key world. She worked hard. It
was a good lesson for David.

Dinner was served late that Sunday. But David did plan,
prepare, and serve it. This middle-class family had a salad and

canned soup. It was not especially good, but it was dinner. He now adds a new dish each month, and he is improving. He does not skip a turn unless he has made a prior arrangement with another family member to switch.

Learning to pay the bills can be another difficult task. You will want to begin by opening a joint bank account with your teen for his money. Teach your teen how to write a check, record it, and balance the account. Having a place to keep incoming bills (in a shoe box on top of the refrigerator) and a set date to pay bills (on the twenty-eighth of each month) will help him form a pattern to follow.

After your young adult child has mastered all of these skills, you may wonder if he will remember to use them before the electricity in his apartment is turned off. Hyperactive children often need help organizing things. You may need to help your young adult start an organization system. A wall calendar with big spaces to write in "Jobs to Be Done" can help.

Allowances Versus Paid Jobs

Psychologists know that hyperactive children need three concepts to be able to learn: **immediate feedback, frequent feedback,** and **consequences.** They know, as every parent of a hyperactive child does, that such children have trouble delaying gratification or waiting for rewards down the road. They live for the immediate moment. When we use tokens and behavioral charts we are using all three of the principles necessary for learning, but how does this translate into your everyday life with your child?

As a parent you will want to forget about giving weekly allowances and other rewards that require "future awareness." Pay the hyperactive child for each task done the moment it is finished. For tasks the child has little or no interest in, you may want to put the token in front of him first.

Max, here's a dollar if you rake all the leaves. Here's fifty cents if you put away all the groceries.

Always pay the child immediately, even if it is a job that has to be divided into parts. For instance, if he has to stack a cord of wood and cannot do it all in one day, you will want to say, "Okay, you'll get fifteen dollars for stacking the whole cord. You've finished about a third of it, so here's your five dollars for the one-third you finished." He is far more likely to finish jobs if he gets rewards immediately and frequently.

It is very important for parents to supervise these children. Parents need to be there to get them started and to encourage them to stay on-task and finish the job they are doing. School can be a losing proposition for the hyperactive child. The Kennedys made the decision to use the same token system for grades that they used for chores. While some people do not believe children should be paid for grades, like most parents, grades were important to the Kennedys, and they paid Max for earning good grades. He knew what the reward was ahead of time: three dollars for an A, two dollars for a B, and one dollar for a C. This was a delayed reward, but they paid him fifty cents for every A paper he brought home. This was an immediate reward. Their son quickly learned that A papers added up to A's on the report card and A's were very profitable.

What to Expect in the Future

Hyperactivity is a disability. While our children cannot be cured, they can do better, and they can work on skills that will help them to become self-supporting and independent adults. Sometimes it helps if we remind ourselves of that. No matter how old your child is, you will want to start rethinking your goals for his future now. Your encouragement or discouragement of your child's interests will play a major role in the goals your child reaches for.

Keeping all of the aspects of this disability in mind, parents need to help their children set realistic goals for themselves. We cannot expect these children to do jobs that require long hours in repetitive, tedious work or to work at a desk all day. If Dad is an engineer, an accountant, or a brain surgeon, in all likelihood his son isn't going to follow in his career footsteps. If your son or daughter is bright and has mild ADHD he or she could own a small business or work with computers. When the time comes, you will want to guide your child's preparation for a career that allows him or her to do a variety of activities and to move around and that offers frequent feedback of some kind.

In a workshop on hyperactivity, Dr. Jeff Sosne, of the Children's Program in Portland, Oregon, encouraged parents and teachers to keep in mind the special needs of this disability when talking to children about jobs they might pursue. He said, "How well a child does in adulthood can depend on how well the child is matched to the career he goes into."[1]

Careers in the entertainment industry, forestry industry, and recreation industry all share the common advantage of jobs that allow workers hands-on work with a lot of movement and variety. Many of the trades also offer hands-on work with movement and variety. Construction workers, cosmetologists, carpenters, plumbers, beauticians, electricians, and masonry workers all enjoy the freedoms hyperactive people need in a job.

If your son or daughter is doing fairly well in school and there is a realistic hope of his attending college, encourage him to learn to work on or with computers. Whether or not he goes into computer science, the computer will play a big part in college success, because it gives feedback immediately and often. Of course there are many careers that require a college degree suitable for adults who have suffered from or still suffer from hyperactivity. These careers should offer the same characteristics desirable in any job a hyperactive individual seeks.

If your son or daughter does decide to go to college, remember that people with ADHD can do the quality of work (grade-level work), but not the quantity. Your son or daughter may need to take an extra year or two to finish college. The workload in college is very heavy, and the ADHD child has problems with large quantities of work. Your child may need to sign up for three courses a semester instead of five. Also, you may need to make some special allowances for a college-bound hyperactive child. You'll want to think about some of the following questions.

- Does he need to live at home so you can supervise?
- Does he have the skills needed to live on his own and complete his work without parental supervision?
- Can he drive a car? Many hyperactive children need to wait a year or two to learn to drive due to problems associated with the disability. Reaching a certain age does not mean they have the skills necessary to become a responsible driver.
- Does he know where and how to find help on campus if he needs it?
- Will he seek help if he needs it?

Choosing a college will be almost as important as choosing a career. ADHD students need smaller classes where their focusing skills will be more successful. We teach them to get involved in discussions, to interact with the teacher and the students. This is almost impossible at a state university, where the average first-year class size is 350 students. The ADHD student may have a miserable time at a university that offers only large classes and very few, if any, backup services for learning-disabled students. You and your son or daughter will have to interview the university carefully. You will want to know all of the following.

- Do they have services for learning-disabled students?
- What size are most of their beginning-level classes?
- Do they have "help" sessions where students can go in small groups?
- Will they allow your child to take his exams on a computer?

These are all questions you may need to ask before sending your child off to college. After you and your child find a college that is a good "match" for him, you will want to remind him that there are some things he can do to increase his chances of success in college.

- Sit in the front so he can form eye contact with the instructor.
- Become involved in the discussions.
- Bring his tape recorder to class and tape all lectures so he will not miss something during an inattentive period.
- Take notes or have a note taker provided.
- Study with a friend who will keep him on-task.
- Take most of his classes when he is freshest.
- Do as much of his work as possible on a computer.

For most hyperactive children, school proves so difficult they are totally discouraged from even considering college. This is fine. Not all "normal" children want to go to college either. You will want to watch your child as he or she grows and develops for any special talents or interests they may have. Can they turn those talents or interests into a career?

If your child like to take pictures, make sure he takes a film class or photography class in high school to see if it is worth pursuing. If your child shows an interest in working with clay, have him or her take a summer pottery class or work with a potter as an assistant.

Throughout childhood and the junior high years, be on the lookout for your child's interests and talents. Encourage them and nurture those interests if there is any chance they can be converted into a paying job your child would enjoy. *Interest* is a key word. ADHD children have a motivation problem. Hyperactive people must be able to maintain an interest in a field to stick to it.

As your child matures, you will want to talk to other team members. Your pediatrician and child psychologist or psychiatrist and the school counselor will all have ideas on areas where your child excels or has interests. Make sure you all share information. As Dr. Sosne said: "A big part of success is matching the hyperactive child to the job."[2]

PART

5

ADHD Young
Adults

12

Outcome: What Happens to Our ADHD Children When They Grow Up?

What happens to hyperactive children when they grow up? Do they finally mature or outgrow hyperactivity? Do they settle down, find partners, marry, raise children, work, and lead normal, productive lives? The question of outcome is important in understanding any disorder.

Outcome as a Spectrum

In this book we have shown that the symptoms of hyperactivity (impulsivity, inattention, and emotional overreacting) express themselves in many areas of the child's life. Most of the problems show up in how the child interacts with other people, be it his teachers, classmates, siblings, or parents. We view outcome as a measure of how successfully (or unsuccessfully) ADHD children adjust and perform in many areas of life. Some of the ADHD children we are going to look at turned out fairly well, while others did not. We will talk about the factors that we think made a difference in how well these children adjusted. We said we view outcome as a spectrum with lots of different degrees between the two extreme points. The young adults we will look at represent various points on that spectrum. While your child may not be exactly like one or the other of these children, you will be able to see similar problems and solutions.

Ted

Ted was first diagnosed with hyperactivity when he was three years and nine months old. He was the fourth child in a family of four children. None of his siblings had hyperactivity. Ted's sister, however, did have learning disabilities. All of the children in Ted's family were very bright, including Ted and his sister with the learning disability.

We considered Ted's degree of ADHD to be in the moderate range; he had problems at school, at home, and with his friends. Once, in second grade, Ted picked up a plank of wood and hit a classmate over the head, opening up a two-inch gash in the other child's forehead. This one incident, which could have been the beginning of conduct disorder, spurred Ted's parents to seek professional help for Ted.

With professional help, Ted's life really started to turn around. He did have to take low doses of medication, Ritalin, and he received weekly sessions with a child psychologist. Ted's parents also made some changes in how they worked with Ted. While his brothers and sister found Ted difficult, they were supportive, and they pulled together with his parents to help as much as they could. They all worked together as a consistent unit. Ted's parents got him interested in an after-school computer club. Club members saw Ted in a setting where Ted always did fairly well. Later in high school, Ted competed in science and technology fairs, helping his team win a state award.

Ted is now twenty-six years old. He graduated from a small private college in his hometown, where his parents live. It took him six years to finish college in computer engineering, but he made it with honors. For the last two years Ted has worked in the high-tech field of computer design and has done well. During high school he went off Ritalin and did fairly well without it. Under the supervision of his psychologist and physician, Ted had to go on very small doses during one year of his college career. He has not had to take Ritalin with his current job, but he and his psychologist have discussed the possibility that he may have to take small doses if advances in his job create changes or if he works on projects that are tedious, lack variety, or are more desk-work-oriented and stressful. Ted knows he has choices. If he does not want to go on medication, he can always turn down promotions that would change his job tasks or change jobs.

All in all, Ted is a success story. He lives a thousand miles from home, has a productive life, maintains his own apartment, and seems happy. So far, he remains unmarried, but he does have friends and family who continue to be emotionally supportive.

Tony

Tony lives at home, but he does so without supervision. It is not that his parents did not try, but they got burned out. Tony was difficult as a preschooler. He had temper tantrums at home, in stores, in restaurants, and while visiting relatives. At school he had great difficulty behaving himself. He fought on the playground and often had to be sent to the principal's office. His schoolwork was below grade level and his potential. He often did not do the work even though he could. His parents tried to discipline Tony but felt they had no success. He argued and resisted when they spoke to him about serious behavior problems. They set expectations about schoolwork, but nothing came of it.

Out of sheer frustration Tony's parents decided that he had to learn from his own mistakes. They stopped asking about schoolwork. They stopped asking where he was going on Friday night or whom he was going to be with. They stopped insisting on an agreed-upon time for Tony to be home. His parents felt angry and disappointed. There was no meaningful exchange between Tony and his parents. Although Tony continues to live at home, he has been rejected. His parents have given up. He was put in jail on two occasions during an eight-year period for what was understated as "conduct-disorder problems." He physically assaulted a boy who owed him money and stole his wallet. He forced a girlfriend into sexual activity when she did not want to have sex (rape). Beyond the two acts that brought about arrests, he committed a dozen or so more that went undetected. Tony is a hyperactive child who acquired a much more serious problem we call conduct disorder.

Conduct Disorder

Conduct disorder means illegal behavior, and it is a serious problem. Children who have conduct disorder show a persistent pattern, not just isolated acts, of behavior that violates the basic rights of others. Physical aggression is common in the disorder. Children may pick fights and may injure the victim. They may destroy property, set fires, or be cruel to animals. They may steal and may mug or threaten to injure others. They may run away from home or be truant from school frequently. They may become promiscuous and force someone into sexual activity.

While we do not mean to imply that Tony should not be held responsible for criminal behavior, we do want to point out that hyperactivity alone did not account for his conduct disorder. Many children who are hyperactive do not end up in jail. There were at least two major problems (hyperactivity was one) that were necessary to tip the balance and sink the ship in Tony's case.

Hyperactivity is known to place children at risk to develop the very serious conduct disorder *if* certain environmental circumstances are in place. Environmental factors seem to be necessary to tip the balance on ADHD children, who are already vulnerable to conduct disorder based on the problem they have with impulsivity, emotional overactivity, and resistance to authority. Such negative environmental factors include parental rejection, inconsistent discipline, multiple changes in family makeup, and psychiatric disorder in a parent.

While Tony was never asked to leave home, his parents were unable to deal with his behavior and were unwilling (or unable) to get help to resolve core problems Tony was having. Essentially, Tony was left without parental guidance.

What Were the Major Differences between Tony and Ted?

We need to look at why Ted turned out very well and Tony did not. Both boys were in the moderate range of hyperactive disorder. Both boys had parents who loved and wanted them when they were born. What were the key things that made the difference in the two boys and how they turned out? Parenting skills. Remember when Ted hit his classmate over the head? Ted could have very well ended up like Tony. He did not because his parents chose to do something at an early age. Ted's parents got professional help; they changed the way they parented Ted, and they never gave up.

It is important for children, including adolescents and teenagers, to *know* that their behavior is monitored. They may resent it, but they need it. As a parent you have the right to know if your child completes homework assignments. You have a right to know where your child goes in the evening and with whom. It is hard for parents to hang in there during the teen years. Parenting a hyperactive child is very difficult, and by the time your child is a teenager you can feel drained and emotionally exhausted. However, when you stop monitoring, you invite trouble.

Sara

Sara was adopted at nine months by well-educated parents. At age three years and four months she was diagnosed as hyperactive by a local pediatrician. Sara had frequent temper tantrums and started to have difficulty with school as early as preschool. She had difficulty listening during story time and difficulty staying seated in circle time. Her first-grade teacher thought Sara was slow, but later testing revealed that she was of normal intelligence but had some learning disabilities. Throughout school, Sara had to struggle. Her two older brothers were top honor students, and playing the role of advocate for Sara was new and sometimes daunting to them. Junior high, with all of its social pressures and demands for more work, was very difficult for Sara. Her parents decided they needed academic help for her and placed her in a private school in a nearby town where she got a lot of one-on-one attention. She also began working with a child psychologist. By her freshman year in high school, Sara was doing fairly well. Then the private school closed and Sara had to reenter the world of public education in a school where most of the kids were bright and had already formed groups. Her mother tried to help by having Sara's friends from the private school over, but for Sara, the biggest problems were academic. Even though Sara attended a learning center at the school, she had a difficult time fitting in. For Sara, every day was a struggle, and for her parents, keeping her in school was a struggle. Sara was happiest at home, working in the kitchen and cooking dinner for her parents. They made a contract. Mom and Dad would pay for Sara to go to cooking school if Sara would finish high school. She did.

Sara is now twenty-two years old, happily married, and doing well in the role of wife and homemaker. In the last few years she has worked successfully as a part-time cook in a hotel. Although she wants children, Sara has postponed pregnancy. She completed high school when it would have been so much easier to drop out, and she never got into trouble with gangs or drugs, despite the fact that "fitting in" in her sophomore year was not easy. Eventually she plans to go to a junior college and major in foods, but she is postponing that until her husband finishes junior college. Considering Sara's multiple disabilities, she is a success story as well.

Kelly Kelly was diagnosed as ADHD at six years of age. School had always been difficult, but she was making passing grades. When she was sixteen years old, she became pregnant. Her initial plans were to quit school and have the baby. After she had the baby she returned home to her mother, father, and fourteen-year-old brother because she had nowhere else to go.

The months during Kelly's pregnancy did not go well with her parents. She had promised to take teen parenting classes but did not. She found the classes "boring," or something would come up and she would cancel out at the last minute. On two occasions during the pregnancy she attended a party and got drunk. She had promised her parents she would not use drugs or alcohol at all during the pregnancy. But she used both at times.

When Kelly came home from the hospital, her parents did not say much to her. But they seemed different. Shortly after returning home she discovered that her parents had packed her things, gotten rid of her dog, and erased all traces of Kelly's life with them by removing all pictures of her from the house. Kelly and her new baby were soon asked to leave. Her parents could not take it anymore; Kelly's behavior had been so unacceptable that they could no longer deal with her. She was rejected. She was ostracized from the family.

Kelly now has five problems:

1. Kelly has problems directly associated with ADHD.
2. She is a parent of a newborn without the maturity or financial and personal resources to cope with the responsibility.
3. She has lost the support (however fragile it was) of her family and other relatives.
4. She is extremely vulnerable to being picked up by predatory males.

5. She is at great risk to start her adult life (as a teen mother) on the poverty track.

Also, Kelly is at risk to show behavior patterns associated with conduct disorder. While girls are less likely than boys to develop antisocial behavior, girls who do may start a pattern of antisocial behavior after age fifteen. **Rejection by family is one of a number of factors that can tip the balance for a vulnerable child.**

Lisa

Like Kelly, Lisa was first diagnosed as ADHD in first grade. Lisa's ADHD was mild; her first-grade teacher did not think that was the problem. She thought Lisa was "a little spoiled and lazy." She thought Lisa's inability to pay attention and overactivity were just "immaturity." But Lisa's mother was a fifth-grade teacher with a specialty in learning disabilities, and she requested a team diagnosis. Lisa's mother's suspicions were correct: Lisa had mild ADHD. Lisa's mother and stepfather worked with her throughout school. While Lisa was bright, she remained a B+ student. Sometime in sixth grade, Lisa announced she wanted to be a doctor. Knowing how difficult a profession this could be for an ADHD individual, Lisa's mother discouraged it. But when her parents saw how persistent Lisa was year after year, they started encouraging her.

Lisa's parents taught her organizational skills and study skills that helped her compensate for her disability, and Lisa made it. She had to work very hard in college, and she had to be twice as organized as most students. Lisa learned to work in chunks, to make lists, and to use the kind of study skills we have talked about in this book. She used a note taker and attended a small college that worked with handicapped students. Lisa's ADHD was mild, and she never needed medication because she could succeed without it. She is now an intern and plans a residency in pediatrics. It has been a struggle for Lisa, too, and her ADHD was mild. Her career choice would not have been possible if she had not had a number of factors working in her favor.

1. Lisa was bright.
2. Lisa had a supportive family.
3. Lisa had mild ADHD.
4. Lisa was willing to do the extra work necessary to compensate for her disability.

All of the children we looked at, the successes and the failures, are on the spectrum. What were the factors that brought about the different outcomes? There are factors we call escalation factors and factors we call protective factors. Escalation factors increase the child's basic vulnerability and make the outcome even worse than what you would expect from an ADHD child. Here is a list of what Dr. Terdal sees as escalation factors that add to the problems of ADHD children.

Escalation Factors

1. *Serious aggressive behavior*—Serious aggressive behavior, especially when it starts early and occurs in several settings, like home, neighborhood, and school, is the single most threatening indicator of serious and long-term problems for ADHD children.
2. *Lack of monitoring by adults*—These children cannot be left to their own devices. Parents who abuse alcohol and other drugs are putting themselves at high risk of being unable to monitor their children effectively. Parents who are overextended, severly depressed, or too involved in their own concerns may be unable to be responsive, supportive, and interested in the day-to-day management of a difficult child.

3. *Lack of consistent and reasonable discipline*—Harsh and inconsistent discipline makes the problems worse. Hyperactive children are at increased risk of being abused. There is no question their behavior is difficult and provocative. They do test the patience of even parents who have a mild temperament and are consistent in discipline matters.

4. *Lack of friends*—Children who are not able to establish relationships with others their age give a subtle but serious signal of poor coping skills. Establishing and keeping friendships is most basic to what we are about.

5. *Failure to learn academic and prevocational skills*—As a psychologist, Dr. Terdal sometimes hears parents make comments like: "I don't care about his academic skills; we need to bring his behavior under control." The comment is usually made in reference to a child who behaves like Dennis the Menace with the volume turned up. Dr. Terdal has never accepted this argument. He feels that we need to keep in mind that part of the task of childhood is preparation for adult living. In the 1990s an adult without academic skills will be at an enormous economic and social disadvantage. Even in cases of children with severe behavior disorders, we must not fail to focus on their learning skills. Otherwise we set them up for later failure. They are the least able to handle additional failures.

Protective Factors

Protective factors are what makes it possible for children with ADHD to do relatively well *in spite* of a vulnerability. Dr. Terdal has a list of five protective factors that give children with ADHD an edge, a better chance.

1. Having parents who *monitor* their child and set limits. Parents who know where their children are, whom they are with, and what they are doing. Parents who set limits

when their child is involved with people or situations that provoke risky antisocial behavior.

2. Having parents who get help and have the resources and supports to be effective as parents. Parents who are not so overwhelmed by their own needs that they cannot consistently track their child.

3. Having parents who discipline *effectively* and *consistently*, using consequences for misbehavior and rewards for positive behavior.

4. Having friends. ADHD children normally have difficulty establishing and maintaining friendships. Problems with sharing, waiting for turns in games, and in such basic social skills as listening can be turnoff for others when ADHD children start friendships. It is often helpful to find interest patterns in the ADHD child and to match them with children with similar interests. Many children do this on their own. ADHD children usually do not. Interests may be music, stamp collecting, or individual sport activities like fishing. Arranging contacts with other children around activities of interest can help form friendships. Asking your child about interests of his companions may help him develop social skills.

5. Having *learned* academic and prevocational skills that will prepare them for adult roles.

There are childhood disorders that are so strongly influenced by biological factors that one defective gene will override all other influences. ADHD is not one of them. ADHD is one disorder where the child's environment can and does make a big difference in how the child will turn out. That is why it is so important to seek help, follow our suggestions for structuring the environment, use the discipline techniques we outline in this book, advocate for your child, and use support groups to keep yourself emotionally strong.

Realistic Expectations of Parenting

Throughout this book, we continually emphasize the importance of giving the child a positive self-concept. Well, your self-concept as a parent is important, too. Just as the hyperactive child constantly suffers blows to his self-esteem, so do parents. As recently as the 1960s, it was thought hyperactivity was caused by bad parenting. Even now, educators, neighbors, and family members may feel free to tell you there is nothing wrong with your child that a good spanking could not cure. Nothing could be further from the truth.

As explained in the early chapters of this book, hyperactivity is related to a physiological difference in the brain. There is a physical reason why our children behave differently. While good parenting can go a long way toward helping your ADHD child, your parenting style did not cause your child to become hyperactive.

Knowing that fact helps, no doubt, but it is still difficult to have a positive view of yourself as a parent when you expect your hyperactive child to respond as "normal" children do. You have to look at this child differently, and you have to look at your expectations of yourself differently, too. You don't have to be a perfect "TV family" with a perfect house and perfect children. What you do have to do is maintain a healthy balance in your life by making time for yourself, your spouse, and your other children. You will also want to redefine parenting, as you can no longer define your success as a parent by how well this child behaves.

PART

6

Just for Parents

CHAPTER 13

Parental Survival:
How to Relieve Stress

The vast majority of this book suggests ways to help your child do better. Any parent who has a hyperactive child will tell you that the better the child does, the better the parents do. If the child has a bad day, Mom and Dad have a bad day, and if the child had a bad week, Mom and Dad have a bad week. If the child has a bad month, Mom and Dad have ulcers. But there are things you can do to make your days better regardless of how your child is doing.

How do parents cope? What can they do to find help and relief? Many parents feel that pulling together as a couple is helpful. Laughter, exercise, prayer, and relaxation are all ways many people relieve their stress. Some parents find that developing outside interests is helpful, while others feel they would not have made it through without professional help from a psychologist or a family counselor. Support groups also offer many parents the emotional support they need to survive the stress.

In this chapter we will discuss different ways parents cope. You may find one method works for you while others do not. Like many parents, you may want to try a combination of methods.

Working Together with Your Spouse

On those days when you find yourself "hating" the child you really love so very much, your spouse is your first line of defense. All too often we hesitate to talk to each other; we are afraid to let our partner know what we are thinking. There are some things you can do to improve your communication with each other.

Verbalize Thoughts and Think Out Loud

It is important to talk to each other, to admit what you are going through, what you are thinking and feeling, and to share your frustrations and successes with each other. Who knows better than your spouse what this child can do to your nerves, not to mention your patience? Your spouse can back up any discipline decisions you may have made, but he can also back up your energy reserves and emotional strengths. Bouncing ideas off each other is important. Sometimes we think of things but are afraid to tell even our partners because we do not want to sound stupid. By bouncing ideas off each other parents may uncover solutions to problems they have worried about for too long. Much to your surprise, you might find your spouse also sees the same problem you do. You will want to bounce ideas off each other for solving problems with your children. For any solution or strategy to work, parents must agree on it.

It is important to set aside time to be with each other. Make an appointment if you have to, but find some way to discuss the events of the day. As we mentioned in Chapter 6, you have to agree on a disciplinary plan, but there may be times when either you or your spouse will disagree on a consequence that one of you gave your child. While it is important not to discuss any disagreement in front of the child, it is very important that you and your spouse discuss it when you are alone together. Mrs. Kennedy shares this experience:

There were many times when, in the heat of anger, I would ground our son for a long period of time. When my husband first learned of the decreed consequence [an agreed-upon grounding], he said nothing in front of our child, but later that night he said, "Don't you think grounding him for a month is a little severe?" After discussing it, we agreed it was too severe. We also agreed we would reward him with three days off his grounding because he was so good at the Boy Scout meeting and five days off his grounding for a B + on his workbook, or something similar.

Your daily "spouse" appointment will do more than keep your discipline going smoothly. It will keep your marriage going smoothly as well.

Periodically you will want to make a longer appointment with each other, for a weekend or a few days together alone, just the two of you. It is important to take a few days away from your hyperactive child and all of the problems you both have to cope with on a daily basis. Occasional weekends alone together will restore your energy, your sanity, and your marriage.

Parenting a hyperactive child can place enormous stress on your marriage. Sometimes we blame each other:

You were hyperactive as a child, I just know it.

Well, how about your father? He is still hyperactive, working two jobs.

Regardless of the cause of your child's hyperactivity, the fact is that you have a hyperactive child and blaming each other does not help the child or you and your spouse and your marriage. If you need to, do not hesitate to seek a marriage counselor. One of the best things you can do for a hyperactive child is raise him in a strong, functional family. Making time for each other is an important part of keeping your marriage together.

This sounds wonderful, but you are thinking, *Who can I get to take care of this child for an entire weekend? Not even his grandparents are wild about taking him for a weekend.* They probably are not, but they will do better if you give them guidance on how to handle your child. Grandparents can do quite well if they are aware of the basic ground rules outlined in the discipline chapter and some other strategies. Be sure to tell Grandpa and Grandma that your ADHD child will do best if he is kept busy. Dr. Russell Barkley points out that hyperactive children do fairly well in certain situations.[1]

- They do best in the early morning instead of later in the day.
- They do best in one-on-one situations.
- They like new, interesting situations.
- They like immediate feedback.

Have Grandma and Grandpa take the kids swimming or to the park, anywhere where the child can release his physical energy. This may carry the added benefit of taking him to places he is not familiar with, so he may find them interesting. Plan activities for them that do not require the child to sit still and listen for long periods of time. You will need to be the one to supply Grandma and Grandpa with ideas. Grandmas and Grandpas are often into winding down, and you are asking them to take charge of the most wound-up individuals around, so help them out with a supply of ideas.

Hyperactive children do best when things remain consistent. If the child has lessons or places he has to go, leave the grandparents with an outline of the child's daily patterns, where he usually goes and when, what he has to do, and when it must be done. Tell them of any token systems you have going and what tokens the child receives. With a little help, Grandma and Grandpa can do quite well.

If Grandma and Grandpa do not work out, there are other solutions. By all means try other, possibly more tolerant family members if you have them. If you belong to a support group for parents of hyperactive children, you may be able to work out an exchange where parents trade off baby-sitting one week-end a month or every two months. Remember, other parents of ADHD children will be as anxious to get away for a weekend as you are.

You might also try putting up a notice at your local college or university in the child psychology or child development de-partment. The college students in these departments like children and usually are very skilled in coping with children, even hyperac-tive children. As always, whenever you leave your children with someone you do not know very well, you will want to check her out carefully, not just her references, but with the university.

While leaving a complicated child with a teenage baby-sitter is not always a good idea, there are exceptions. If you know the sitter well and know that she is responsible, capable of handling your child, and in touch with adult backup, then that, too, can be an option. When you find a good sitter, you will want to keep her for as long as possible. We found the best way to do this was to pay them more than the current going rate for sitters. Extra money goes a long way toward helping the sitter forget the extra effort she must make while taking care of your child.

Raising a hyperactive child is a stressful situation, and stress for any reason can take its toll on the strongest marriages. For that reason, putting forth the extra effort to communicate and share time and encouragement with your spouse is so worth-while. Yes, working on your marriage, like working with your hyperactive child, does require time and some energy, but any family counselor will tell you that the emotional cost of a divorce is much higher.

When You Think You Are Going to Cry, Try Laughing

Please know that every parent alive who has actually raised a hyperactive child has, at one time or another, disliked that child intensely. Usually this intense dislike comes immediately after the child has done something thoughtless and impulsive, like using the printout of your research paper to clean up the puppy poo. Laughter is good medicine, and it goes a long way toward relieving stress. While it is hard to laugh when some of these things are actually happening, it is vital that you keep your sense of humor while raising your hyperactive child. Almost any humorous book will help relieve the bottled-up tension you may be feeling. When you go to the movies, see comedies, not the depressing tragedies.

Most important, develop a new attitude toward life. Look for the humor in situations. When you feel like you could explode, ask yourself if this could possibly be funny in five or ten years. Imagine yourself telling your mother or friends about the incident sometime in the future. It could turn out like the following example when Pat Kennedy's mother came to visit:

A Lesson in Laughter   You know my friend Jane, who takes Max for me, Mom? Well, the other day I watched her three kids for her while she went to the doctor. All five kids were playing well when the phone rang. While I was on the phone for two seconds with another friend, the doorbell rang and it was two of the neighborhood kids, one of whom is also hyperactive. They wanted to show Max and Jane's son the salamanders they had just caught at the pond in the park. They had them in these little tiny sour cream cups that could not have been more than one inch deep. Can you imagine, Mom? Those boys had on rubber hip boots, and they were caked with mud, and they wanted to come in. I told them they had to take the boots off and that their shaggy dog, Moppy, had to stay outside. I shouldn't have left the door opened while I told them that, because that dog saw our cat and a high-speed chase ensued through the house. The muddy dog followed the cat and the boys followed the dog, over the sofa, up the stairs, and into the kitchen, where the cat climbed the drapes on the patio door and hung there while the dog barked at him below. Those boys just left the salamanders in those little cups on the floor in the front hall when they went to catch Moppy. Well, I just about had the dog and the boys out the door when they discovered the salamanders were missing and all hell broke loose. I never did say good-bye to my friend on the phone.

As Pat's mother was the parent of two well-behaved girls who were not hyperactive this story brought little more than a smile: she did not laugh but responded, "How could you let such a thing happen?" The words had no sooner left her mouth when Max came down the stairs, grabbed the tassel on the bottom of a plant hanger, and tried to swing across the living room yelling, "Geronimo!" As the plant, the plant hanger, a chunk of plaster wall, and Max all fell to the floor, Pat looked at her mom and said, "Mom, how could you let such a thing happen?" They both had a good laugh.

While Pat did not laugh when she cleaned the mud from her sofa and carpets or repaired the drapes in the kitchen, she did realize that what had happened was not tragic; it was just a lot of work. Having Max do his part in the cleanup by vacuuming helped, but it was not until her husband, who was not involved in the cleanup, came home and got a good laugh out of the whole incident that she began to realize that the whole episode was really funny.

Develop Outside Interests

Outside interests can go a long way toward providing some relief from stress. Anything from cross-stitch to cooking classes can offer parents a source of interest and accomplishment. Diversions like crafts, hobbies, classes, and projects are all activities many parents find interesting and even relaxing. They help to relieve stress in a number of ways. They take our minds off our problems, and they offer us a more controlled situation with a high likelihood of success. These activities not only occupy our minds, but they reward us with a sense of satisfaction that can only bolster our emotional well-being. Turning a hobby or a craft into a money-producing venture provides additional stress-relieving benefit: It can relieve stress by providing a source of extra income, which in turn can be used for sitters, counselors, recreation, or other extras we often feel we cannot afford. A word of caution: Never allow your outside interest to become stressful. One woman crocheted dolls as a hobby and found it very relaxing. An additional benefit of selling the dolls at Christmas bazaars turned into a nightmare when she accepted an order for fifteen dolls shortly before the holidays. Keep your hobby as a stress reliever, not a stress producer.

For many parents, outside interests may consist of their job and work-related activities. Jobs outside the home provide parents with another area to focus on, something to think about and work on besides their hyperactive child. They can offer parents a sense of accomplishment and rewards that they do not always get from parenting a difficult child. With a job, parents can see some achievements at the end of every day. Working with a hyperactive child can take weeks and months before achievements are noticeable. Outside jobs also can give the parents an emotional and physical break from dealing with their child. This is true especially if parents have good child care and the caregiver is cooperative in following the disciplinary plan. If being a two-income family is not a necessity, parents will want to weigh the pros and cons carefully. While working outside the home can be very helpful, it can become a source of stress. Careful management of your time and attention to details, like making sure you have a backup sitter in case of illness, will go a long way toward relieving work-related stress.

Exercise

Whether you are a stay-at-home or working parent, you will definitely find exercise an excellent way to reduce the stress you feel. Daily exercise will improve your physical and mental fitness level. Exercise has been shown to reduce blood pressure, cholesterol, and weight, but it also increases stamina and overall good health. If parents put aside time to jog or take a brisk walk every morning together, they can compound the dividend. While it is wonderful to exercise as a couple, some parents with conflicting schedules find exercise an enjoyable activity they can each do separately with their hyperactive child. Walking, swimming, or biking with your ADHD child daily will do a lot for both of you. Exercising together can be a positive experience you can share while burning off the child's energy and the parent's stress.

Practice Affirmations

Affirmations really are the power of positive thinking. Like the little engine that could, if you think you can do it, you can. Affirmations can be helpful to both parents and children. Saying to yourself, "I will be patient; I will not lose my cool," can help you to think and react more positively toward your child. In doing so you will retain your patience and "cool" that escapes you so often.

You can use this technique with your child as well. Sending your child out the door each morning with a kiss and the affirmation: "You will catch the bus on time," or "You will remember to hand in your homework" can serve as a successful reminder. Affirmations that build self-confidence can be even more helpful to children. Reminding your ADHD child that he is smart and can succeed will help him to believe in his ability and succeed.

Relax

Remember when you had the child who is now causing stress? Well, many of us took a natural childbirth class where we learned Lamaze or Bradley relaxation techniques. Although you may have pushed everything even remotely connected to pregnancy to the back of your mind, relaxation techniques are well worth remembering. You may want to try a modified version of relaxation techniques daily. When you feel yourself tensing up, lie down or sit down. Visualize yourself somewhere very relaxing, the beach or a mountaintop, for example. Imagine the cool waves of water or air washing gently over you. Take deep cleansing breaths, breathing in *one, two, three,* and out *one, two, three.* Start to relax your whole body, first your toes, then your ankles. Let them go totally limp. Relax your legs, your body, your arms, and your head and your mind. If you can fall asleep for five minutes, so much the better. When I tried this in the daytime, a child would invariably jump on my stomach just as I was falling asleep, but if you do it at night it works very well.

Pray and Meditate

For many people prayer is very relaxing, and it certainly deserves mention as a way to relieve stress. It does not matter what faith you are or whether you attend religious services; for that matter, you do not have to be in a church to pray. There is something very calming about prayer and meditation. Daily prayer or meditation can lift your spirits and give you faith in the future and a perspective on the past. Somehow in prayer you realize this, too, shall pass and in the universal scheme of things all the little annoying things your child has done and will do are not all that earth-shattering. Having a church or synagogue where members are emotionally supportive of you and your family is an extra bonus.

Attend Support Group Meetings

Certainly, support groups can play a major role in helping parents cope with the stress of raising a hyperactive child. You will meet other parents who have shared your concerns, your trials, and your experiences. Knowing that you are not the first or the only parent to go through this is enormously helpful. If you have never been to a support group, you may wonder what they do. Support groups get together, usually in an informal setting, and offer parents an opportunity to talk about their experiences and frustrations in dealing with their ADHD child. Many groups will pool resources and bring in speakers with expertise on ADHD, like doctors, psychologists, or even pharmacists. Educational programs sponsored by support groups educate not only parents of ADHD children, but also the community.

In the informal setting of a support group, parents can exchange information on doctors (who is willing to work with a team and who is not) and other professionals. Parents will freely exchange information on resources they have found—physical therapists, baby-sitters, and community programs that are helpful to ADHD children—and other information that might take months for a parent to learn on his own. Support groups offer another valuable feature. Most groups have a monthly or bimonthly newsletter. Newsletters bring members up to date on the latest news on ADHD, speakers, or programs that may be coming up, and services that are available. Moveover, newsletters link members together, even those who can't attend meetings.

Probably the most valuable service a support group offers is emotional support. In a support group others will listen to you, they will encourage you when your are discouraged, and most of all, they will understand. They have walked in your shoes.

Be Good to Yourself

Being kind to yourself and your body should include the basics and then some. Basics include getting enough sleep and exercise and eating a good diet. Diets full of junk food and sugar play havoc with your blood sugar and your weight. Having too much of either blood sugar or weight is bound to depress you, and depression is something you do not need. If you eat a good, healthy diet, full of fresh vegetables and fruits and lean meats, low in fat and high in fiber, you will feel better and you will be more capable of handling the difficult days.

Stay away from too much coffee, sugar, and caffeine. All of these can seem soothing, but ultimately they may jangle your nerves, and you have already got someone to add excitement to your life. Parents, pamper yourself with a night out, a golf game, a new hair-style, any of the little things that make you feel good about yourself. Be sure to allow some luxury, too. Fathers can come home from a fishing trip feeling as if they can succeed at just about anything. How hard can it be to raise a hyperactive child when you have just caught the only two-foot trout in the whole lake?

Raising a hyperactive child can be so difficult that many parents slowly slip into using alcohol and prescription drugs "to help them cope." Far from helping, alcohol and other drugs will reduce your ability to cope as a parent, and ultimately they will become a bigger problem with which you must cope. Alcohol and other drugs do not help you cope; they help you to pretend you are escaping. But the problems are still there, and they are usually intensified and worsened by substance abuse.

Find Some Helpful Philosophies to Live By

It has long been thought that being philosophical about life leads to serenity. Looking at life with your hyperactive child always requires perspective, and putting things in perspective every day indeed will help you feel better about your life.

Of course it is always important to remember how much you love your child, but when he does something impulsive or destructive it can be difficult. **When you are feeling angry or upset with your child, stop and make a mental list of all of his good qualities.** It is easier to calm down and forgive a child who had just dismantled your sewing machine when you remind yourself that he is kind, he is generous, and he is mechancially inclined: he will put it back together. Remember another philosophy: **Nothing looks as bad in the calm of tomorrow as it does in the heat of today.** Yes, the child is responsible for his actions, and he must either fix the sewing machine, pay for it to be fixed, or replace it. Try and work out a solution with the child. Can he fix it? Can he work off the cost of the repairs by doing chores? Can he pay for a used sewing machine from a garage sale?

Remaining philosophical about your sewing machine is not easy when it is on the floor in twenty pieces and you have to have costumes for the school play finished by next week, but you should ask yourself: *Will this be important in fifteen years?* Surely you will have forgotten the costumes and the fact that your sewing machine was in twenty pieces by fifteen years from now.

Frustrations with school and social problems are much harder to be philosophical about. You worry about how your child is going to manage a job when he does not remember to hand in his homework or if he will quit his job because he is so impulsive. Sometimes you wonder if he will end up living under the bridge or living with you. If you are working on skills that will help him remember to hand in his homework and he is working on controlling his impulsive behavior, then have faith: **This, too,**

shall improve. Sixty to 70 percent of these children will grow up to be self-supporting adults who can live on their own.

Always Look at How Far Your Child Has Come, Not How Far He Has to Go

Hyperactive children make progress very slowly, one step forward and two steps back. At times it can seem overwhelming and depressing. We look at it from an adult perspective and think of all the things he still has not mastered that he will need to function as an adult. We are concerned because he is in third grade and still has trouble making friends or difficulty paying attention. First, you need to know that not all "normal" children his age have mastered the tasks that escape our children. Then you will want to look at all of the things he has mastered. Remember when he was only four and you wondered if he would even survive the school system? When we look back, we can see how many strides our children have made and how much they have accomplished. The future is full of uncertainty, and it is frightening to think of your child with his present level of skills coping in today's world. Try to remember that he will not have to cope with his present level of skills; he has time to learn more skills, one day at a time. You and your team have time to teach him, and working together you can accomplish more than you realize.

Gaining a new perspective on your situation can prove difficult for even the highly skilled parent. Working with a child psychologist can help your child to gain a new perspective on family life and his place in it. A good child psychologist not only offers parents fresh ideas on coping with their child; he offers the child some insight and ideas on ways to change his behavior.

We hope this book has given *you* insight and ideas on living with an ADHD child. What you do *does* make a difference.

Notes

Chapter 1

1. Levine, M. D., Brooks, R. and Shonkoff, J. P. (1980).
   A Pediatric Approach to Learning Disorders. New York:
   John Wiley & Sons, p. 52.
2. Shaywitz, S. E. and Shaywitz, B. A. (1991). Introduction
   to the special series on attention deficit disorder. *Journal
   of Learning Disabilities, 24,* 68–71.
3. Levine, M. D. (1987). *Developmental Variation and
   Learning Disorders.* Cambridge, MA: Educators Publishing Service, 36.
4. Wender, Paul, *The Hyperactive Child, Adolescent, and
   Adult.* New York: Oxford University Press, 1987, p. 19.
   See also Barkley, Russell A., "Attention Deficit-Hyperactivity Disorder," a workshop manual for clinicians.
   University of Massachusetts pub., 1990, p. 8.
5. Levine, M. D. (1987). *Developmental Variation and
   Learning Disorders.* Cambridge, MA: Educators Pub-
   lishing Service, 409.
   Barkley, R. A. (1990). *Attention Deficit Hyperactivity
   Disorder: A Handbook for Diagnosis and Treatment.*
   New York: Guilford Press.
6. Levine, M. D., Brooks, R., and Shonkoff, J. P. (1980).
   A Pediatric Approach to Learning Disorders. Philadelphia:
   John Wiley & Sons, 58.
7. Levine, M. D. (1987). *Developmental Variation and*

Learning Disorders. Cambridge, MA: Educators Publishing Service.

8. Thomas, A., and Chess, S. (1963). *Behavioral Individuality in Early Childhood.* New York: New York University Press.

Chapter 2

1. Jensen, J. B., and Garfinkel, B. D. (1988). Neuroendocrine aspects of attention deficit hyperactivity disorders. *Neurologic Clinics, 6,* 111–29.

2. Shekim, W. O., Dekirmenjian, H., Chapel, J. L., Javaid, J., and Davis, J. M. (1979). Norepinephrine metabolism and clinical response to dextroamphetamine in hyperactive boys. *Journal of Pediatrics, 95,* 389–394.

3. Hartsough, C., and Lambert, N. M. (1985). Medical factors in hyperactive and normal children: Prenatal, developmental and healthy history findings. *American Journal of Orthopsychiatry, 55,* 190–201.
   Levine, M. D., Brooks, R., and Shonkoff, J. P. (1980). *A Pediatric Approach to Learning Disorders.* Philadelphia: John Wiley and Sons.

4. David, O., Clark, J., and Voeller, K. (1972). Lead and hyperactivity. *Lancet,* 900–3.
   David, O. J., Hoffman, P. S., Sverd, J., and Clark, J. (1977). Lead and hyperactivity: Lead levels among hyperactive children. *Journal of Abnormal Child Psychology, 5,* 405–16.

5. Gross-Tsur, V., Shelev, R. S., and Amir, N. (1991). Attention deficit disorder: Association with Familial-Genetic factors. *Pediatric Neurology, 7,* 258–61.

6. Biederman, J., Munir, K., Knee, D., Habelow, M. A., Armentano, M., Autor, S., Hoge, S. K., and Waternaux, C. (1986). A family study of patients with attention deficit disorder and normal controls. *Journal of Psychiatric Research, 20,* 263–74.

7. Wolraich, M., Tumbo, P. J., Milich, R., Chenard, C., Shultz, F., 1986, Dietary Characteristics of Hyperactive and Control Boys. *Journal of the American Nutrition*

and Dietetic Association, 86, 500–4.

Barkley, R. A. (1990). *Attention Deficit Hyperactivity Disorder: A Handbook for Diagnosis and Tretment.* New York: Guilford Press.

8. Feingold, B. (1975). *Why Your Child Is Hyperactive.* New York: Random House.

9. Feingold, B. F. (1976). Hyperkinesis and learning disabilities linked to the ingestion of artificial foods and flavors. *Journal of Learning Disabilities, 9*, 551–59.

10. Goyette, C. H., Conners, C. K., Petti, T. A., and Curtis, L. (1978). Effects of artificial colors on hyperkinetic children: A double-blind challenge study. *Psychopharmacology Bulletin, 14*, 39–40.

    Harley, J. P., Ray, R. S., Tomasi, L., Eichman, P. L., Matthews, C. G., Chun, R., Cleeland, C. S., and Traisman, E. (1981). Hyperkinesis and food additives: Testing the Fcingold hypothesis. *Pediatrics, 61*, 818–28.

    Kaplan, B., McNicol, J., Conte, R., and Moghadam, H. (1989). Dietary replacement in pre-school hyperactive and normal boys. *Pediatrics, 83*, 7–17.

    Mattes, J. A., and Gittelman-Klein, R. (1981). Effects of artificial food colorings in children with hyperactive symptoms: A critical review and results of a controlled study. *Archives of General Psychiatry, 38*, 714–18.

    Palmer, S., Rapoport, J. L., and Quinn, P. O. (1975). Food additives and hyperactivity. *Clinical Pediatrics, 14*, 956–59.

    Wender, E. (1986). The food additive–free diet in the treatment of behavior disorders: A review. *Journal of Developmental and Behavioral Pediatrics, 7*, 35–42.

    Williams, J. I., and Cram, D. M. (1978). Diet in the management of hyperkinesis: A review of the tests of Feingold's hypothesis. *Canadian Psychiatric Association Journal, 23*, 241–48.

11. United States National Institutes of Health. (1982). Consensus conference: defined diets and childhood hyperactivity. *Journal of American Medical Association, 248*, 290–92.

12.   Bock, S. A. (1987). Prospective appraisal of complaints
      of adverse reactions to foods in children during the first
      three years of life. *Pediatrics, 79*, 683–88.

      McMahon, R. C. (1981). Biological factors in childhood
      hyperkinesis: A review of genetics and biochemical hy-
      pothesis. *Journal of Clinical Psychology, 37*, 12–21.

      Milich, R., Loney, J., and Landau, S. (1982). Inde-
      pendent dimensions of hyperactivity and aggression: A
      validation with playroom observation data. *Journal of
      Abnormal Psychology, 91*, 183–98.

Chapter 3

1.   Levine, M.D., Carey, W.B., Crocker, A.C., and Gross
     R.T. (eds.) (1983). *Developmental Behavioral Pediatrics.*
     Philadelphia: W. B. Saunders, p. 229.
2.   Thomas, A. (1965). Significance of temperamental indi-
     viduality for school functioning. In J. Hellmuth (ed.),
     Learning Disorders, Vol. 3. Seattle: Special Child Pub-
     lications, 347–56.

     Thomas, A., and Chess, S. (1963). *Behavioral Individ-
     uality in Early Childhood.* New York: New York Uni-
     versity Press.

     Thomas, A., and Chess, S. (1977). *Temperament and
     Development.* New York: Brunner-Mazel.

     Thomas, A., and Chess, S. (1980). *Dynamics of Psycho-
     logical Development.* New York: Brunner-Mazel.
3.   Levine, M. D., Brooks, R., and Shonkoff, J. P. (1980).
     A Pediatric Approach to Learning Disorders. Philadelphia:
     John Wiley & Sons.

Chapter 4

1.   Dulcan, M. K. (1985). The psychopharmacologic treat-
     ment of children and adolescents with attention deficit
     disorder. *Psychiatric Annals, 15*, 69–86.

     Shekim, W. O., Dekirmenjian, H., Chapel, J. L., Javaid,
     J., and Davis, J. M. (1979). Norepinephrine metabolism

and clinical response to dextroamphetamine in hyperactive boys. *Journal of Pediatrics, 95,* 389–94.

2. Rapoport, J., Buchsbaum, M., Weingartner, H., Zahn, R., Ludlow, C., and Mickkelsen, E. (1980). Dextroamphetamine: Its cognitive and behavioral effects in normal and hyperactive boys and normal men. *Archives of Journal of Psychiatry, 37,* 933–43.

3. Barkley, R. A. (1990). *Attention Deficit Hyperactivity Disorder: A Handbook for Diagnosis and Treatment.* New York: Guilford Press.

   Barkley, R. A., McMurray, M. B., Edelbrock, C. S., and Robbins, K. (1990). The side effects of methylphenidate in children with attention hyperactivity disorder: A systemic, placebo-controlled evaluation. *Pediatrics, 86,* 184–92.

Chapter 5

1. Lindgren, H. C. (1967). *Educational Psychology in the Classroom.* New York: John Wiley and Sons.

Chapter 6

1. Barkley, R. A. (1990). *Attention Deficit Hyperactivity Disorder: A Handbook for Diagnosis and Treatment.* New York: Guilford Press, 79.

   Levine, M. D. (1987). *Developmental Variation and Learning Disorders.* Cambridge, MA: Educators Publishing Service, 409.

Chapter 8

1. Barkley, R. A. (1988). *Attention Deficit Hyperactivity Disorders: Diagnosis, Assessment and Treatment.* Handbook given as part of a presentation on April 1, 1988, to the University Affiliated Program, Child Development and Rehabilitation Center, Oregon Health Sciences University, Portland.

   Barkley, R. A. (1990). "Attention Deficit-Hyperactivity

Disorder," a workshop manual for clinicians, University of Massachusetts Pub. 55 Lake Avenue North, Worcester, MA 01655.

Chapter 9

1. Zametkin, A. J., Nordahl, T. E., and Gross, M. (1990). Cerebral glucose metabolism in adults with hyperactivity of childhood onset. *New England Journal of Medicine, 323*, 1361–66.

Chapter 10

1. U.S. Office of Education. (1986). First annual report, National Advisory on Handicapped Children. Washington, D.C.: U.S. Department of Health, Education and Welfare.

Chapter 11

1. Sosne, J. (1990). *How to Work with a Hyperactive Child in School.* Portland: Children's Program, 5331 SW Macadam, Suite 210, Portland, OR 97201. (Handouts at workshop on October 12, 1990.)
2. Sosne, J. (1990). *How to Work with a Hyperactive Child in School.* Portland: Children's Program, 5331 SW Macadam, Suite 210, Portland, OR 97201. (Handouts at workshop on October 12, 1990.)

Chapter 13

1. Barkley, R. A. (1988). *Attention Deficit Hyperactivity Disorders: Diagnosis, Assessment and Treatment.* Handbook given as part of a presentation on April 1, 1988, to the University Affiliated Program, Child Development and Rehabilitation Center, Oregon Health Sciences University, Portland.

References

Accardo, P. J. Blondis, T. A., and Whitman, B. Y. (eds.) (1991). *Attention Deficit Disorders and Hyperactivity in Children*. New York: Marcel Dekker.

Achenbach, T., and Edelbrock, C. S. (1983). *Manual for the Child Behavioral Checklist and Revised Child Behavior Profile*. Burlington: University of Vermont, Department of Psychiatry.

Baldessarini, R. J. (1972). Symposium: Behavior modificaton by drugs: 1. Pharmacology of amphetamines. *Pediatrics, 49,* 694–708.

Barkley, R. A. (1977a). A review of stimulating drug research with hyperactive children. *Journal of Child Psychology and Psychiatry, 18,* 137–65.

Barkley, R. A. (1977b). The effects of methylphenidate on various types of activity level and attention in hyperkinetic children. *Journal of Abnormal Psychology, 5,* 351–69.

Barkley, R. A. (1982). Specific guidelines for defining hyperactivity in children: Attention deficit disorder with hyperactivity. In B. Lahey and A. Kazdin (eds)., *Advances in Clinical Child Psychology*. New York: Plenum, 137–80.

Barkley, R. A. (1988). *Attention Deficit Hyperactivity Disorders: Diagnosis, Assessment and Treatment*. Handbook given as part of a presentation on April 1, 1988, to the University Affiliated Program, Child Development and Rehabilitation Center, Oregon Health Sciences University, Portland.

Barkley, R. A. (1990). *Attention Deficit Hyperactivity Disorder: A Handbook for Diagnosis and Treatment*. New York: Guilford Press.

Barkley, R. A., Anastopolous, A. D., Guevremont, D. C., and Fletcher, K. E. (1991). Adolescents with ADHD: Patterns of behavioral adjustment, academic functioning, and treatment utilization. *Journal of American Academy of Child and Adolescent Psychiatry*, 30, 752–61.

Barkley, R. A., and Cunningham, C. (1979a). The effects of methylphenidate on mother-child interactions of hyperactive children. *Archives of General Psychiatry*, 36, 201–8.

Barkley, R. A., and Cunningham, C. (1979b). Stimulant drugs and activity level in hyperactive children. *American Journal of Orthopsychiatry*, 49, 491–99.

Barkley, R. A., and Cunningham, C. (1980). The parent-child interactions of hyperactive children and their modification by stimulant drugs. In R. E. Knights and D. J. Bakker (eds.), *Treatment of Hyperactive and Learning Disordered Children*. Baltimore: University Press, 219–36.

Barkley, R. A., and McMurray, M. B., Edelbrock, C. S., and Robbins, K. (1989). The response of aggressive and nonaggressive ADHD children to two doses of methylphenidate. *American Academy of Child and Adolescent Psychiatry*, 28, 873–81.

Barkley, R. A., McMurray, M. B., Edelbrock, C. S., and Robbins, K. (1990). The side effects of methylphenidate in children with attention deficit hyperactivity disorder: A systemic, placebo-controlled evaluation. *Pediatrics*, 86, 184–92.

Biederman, J., Munir, K., Knee, D., Habelow, M. A., Armentano, M., Autor, S., Hoge, S. K., and Waternaux, C. (1986). A family study of patients with attention deficit disorder and normal controls. *Journal of Psychiatric Research*, 20, 263–74.

Bock, S. A. (1987). Prospective appraisal of complaints of adverse reactions to foods in children during the first three years of life. *Pediatrics*, 79, 683–88.

Campbell, S. B., Breaux, A. M., Ewing, L. J., and Szumowski, E. K. (1986). Correlates and predictors of hyperactivity and aggression: A longitudinal study of parent-referred problem preschoolers. *Journal of Abnormal Child Psychology*, 14, 217–34.

Cantwell, D. P. (1985). Hyperactive children have grown up. *Archives of General Psychiatry*, 42, 1026–28.

Cantwell, D. P., and Baker, L. (1987). Differential diagnosis of hyperactivity. *Journal of Developmental and Behavioral Pediatrics*, 8, 159–70.

Carey, W. B. (1990a). Temperament risk factors in children: A conference report. *Journal of Developmental and Behavioral Pediatrics*, *11*, 28–34.

Carey, W. B. (1990b). Temperament Difference in Children. *Early Childhood Update*, Vol. *6*, 1–3.

Chess, S., and Thomas, A. (1983). Individuality: Dynamics of individual behavior development. In M. D. Levine, W. B. Carey, A. C. Crocker, and R. T. Gross (eds.), *Developmental-Behavioral Pediatrics*. Philadelphia: W. B. Saunders, 158–75.

Conners, C. K. (1990). *Manual for Conners' Rating Scales*. North Tonawanda, NY: Multi-Health Systems.

Conners, C. K., and Barkley, R. A. (1969). Rating scales and checklists for child psychopharmacology. *Psychopharmacology Bulletin*, *21*, 809–12.

Cunningham, C., and Barkley, R. A. (1978a). The effects of methylphenidate on the mother-child interactions of hyperactive twin boys. *Developmental Medicine and Child Neurology*, *20*, 634–42.

Cunningham, C., and Barkley, R. A. (1978b). The role of academic failure in hyperactive behavior. *Journal of Learning Disorders*, *2*, 15–21.

Cunningham, C., and Barkley, R. A. (1979). The interactions of hyperactive and normal children with their mothers in free play and structured tasks. *Child Development*, *50*, 217–24.

David, O., Clark, J., and Voeller, K. (1972). Lead and hyperactivity. *Lancet*, 900–3.

David, O. J., Hoffman, P. S., Sverd, J., and Clark, J. (1977). Lead and hyperactivity: Lead levels among hyperactive children. *Journal of Abnormal Child Psychology*, *5*, 405–16.

Denckla, M. B., LeMay, M., and Chapman, C. A. (1985). Few CT scan abnormalities found even in neurologically impaired learning disabled children. *Journal of Learning Disabilities*, *18*, 132–35.

Denckla, M. B., and Rudel, R. G. (1978). Anomalies of motor development in hyperactive boys. *Annals of Neurology*, *3*, 183–87.

Douglas, V. I., Barr, R. G., Amin, K., O'Neil, M. E., and Briton, B. G. (1980). Dosage effects and individual responsivity to methylphenidate in attention deficit disorder. *Journal of Child Psychology and Psychiatry and Allied Disciplines*, *29*, 453–75.

Dulcan, M. K. (1985). The psychopharmacologic treatment of children and adolescents with attention deficit disorder. *Psychiatric Annals,* *15,* 69–86.

Feingold, B. (1975). *Why Your Child Is Hyperactive.* New York: Random House.

Feingold, B. F. (1976). Hyperkinesis and learning disabilities linked to the ingestion of artificial foods and flavors. *Journal of Learning Disabilities, 9,* 551–59.

Gammon, G. D. (1992). Fluoxetine appears to help curb refractory ADD: A sampling of reports from annual meeting of the American Academy of Child and Adolescent Psychiatry in San Francisco. *Pediatric News, 26,* 18.

Gittelman-Klein, R., Klein, D. F., Abikoff, H., Katz, S., Gloisten, A. C., and Kates, W. (1976). Relative efficacy of methylphenidate and behavior modification in hyperkinetic children: An interim report. *Journal of Abnormal Child Psychology, 4,* 316–79.

Goyette, C. H., Conners, C. K., Petti, T. A., and Curtis, L. (1978). Effects of artificial colors on hyperkinetic children: A double-blind challenge study. *Psychopharmacology Bulletin, 14,* 39–40.

Harley, J. P., Ray, R. S., Tomasi, L., Eichman, P. L., Matthews, C. G., Chun, R., Cleeland, C. S., and Traisman, E. (1981). Hyperkinesis and food additives: Testing the Feingold hypothesis. *Pediatrics, 61,* 818–28.

Harsough, C., and Lambert, N. M. (1985). Medical factors in hyperactive and normal children: Prenatal, developmental and health history findings. *American Journal of Orthopsychiatry, 55,* 190–201.

Henker, B., and Whalen, C. (1989). Hyperactivity and attention deficits. *American Psychologist, 44,* 216–23.

Jensen, J. B., and Garfinkel, B. D. (1988). Neuroendocrine aspects of attention deficit hyperactivity disorder. *Neurologic Clinics, 6,* 111–29.

Kaplan, B., McNicol, J., Conte, R., and Moghadam, H. (1989). Dietary replacement in pre-school hyperactive and normal boys. *Pediatrics, 83,* 7–17.

Kaplan, H. I., and Sadock, B. J. (1980). Chapter 40, "Tic Disorders," in A. Freeman, H. Kaplan, and B. Sadock, (eds.), *Comprehensive Textbook of Psychiatry,* vol. 2, 5th ed. New York: Plenum Publications.

Kinsbourne, M. (1974). Disorders of mental development. In J. H. Menkes (ed.), *Textbook of Child Neurology.*

Kinsbourne, M., and Caplan, P. J. (1979). *Children's Learning and Attention Problems.* Boston: Little, Brown.

Klein, R. G., and Mannuzza, S. (1991). Long-term outcome of hyperactive children: A review. *Journal of American Academy of Child and Adolescent Psychiatry, 30,* 383–87.

Lahey, B. B., Green, K. D., and Forchand, R. (1980). On the independence of ratings of hyperactivity, conduct problems and attention deficits in children: A multiple regression analysis. *Journal of Consulting and Clinical Psychology, 48,* 566–74.

Lahey, B., Schaughency, E., Strauss, C., and Frame, C. (1984). Are attention deficit disorders with and without hyperactivity similar or dissimilar disorders? *Journal of the American Academy of Child Psychiatry, 23,* 302–9.

Leidel, J. (1990). Information for parents of children who are taking medication for attention deficit-hyperactivity disorder. Handout, Children's Program, 5331 SW Macadam, Portland, OR.

Levine, M. D. (1987). *Developmental Variation and Learning Disorders.* Cambridge, MA: Educators Publishing Service.

Levine, M. D., Brooks, R., and Shonkoff, J. P. (1980). *A Pediatric Approach to Learning Disorders.* New York: John Wiley & Sons.

Levine, M. D., Carey, W. B., Crocker, A. C., and Gross, R. T. (eds.) (1983). *Developmental Behavioral Pediatrics.* Philadelphia: W. B. Saunders.

Lewis, M., and Taft, L. T. (1982). *Developmental Disabilities: Theory, Assessment and Intervention.* New York: SP Medical and Scientific Books.

Liden, C. B., Laurie, T. E., and Porter, C. J. (1982). *Issues in Developmental Pediatrics,* vol. 4. The Department of Pediatrics, University of Pittsburgh and the Children's Hospital of Pittsburgh.

Lindgren, H. C. (1967). *Educational Psychology in the Classroom.* New York: John Wiley and Sons.

Linnoila, M., Gaultieri, C. T., Jobson, K., and Staye, L. J. (1979). Characteristics of the therapeutic response to imipramine in hyperactive children. *American Journal of Psychiatry, 136,* 1201–203.

Loney, J. (1987). Hyperactivity and aggression in the diagnosis of attention deficit disorder. In B. B. Lahey and A. D. Kazdin (eds.),

Advances in Clinical Child Psychology, vol. 10. New York: Plenum Press.

Loney, J., Langhorne, J. E., and Paternite, C. E. (1978). An empirical basis for subgrouping the hyperkinetic/minimal brain syndrome. *Journal of Abnormal Psychology, 87*, 431–41.

Mannuzza, S., Klein, R. G., and Addalli, K. A. (1991). Young adult mental status of hyperactive boys and their brothers: A prospective follow-up study. *Journal of American Academy of Child and Adolescent Psychiatry, 30*, 743–51.

Mash, E. J., and Barkley, R. A. (1989). *Behavioral Treatment of Childhood Disorders.* New York: Guilford Press.

Mash, E. J., Johnston, C., and Kovitz, K. (1983). A comparison of the mother-child interactions of physically abused and non–physically abused children during play and task situations. *Journal of Clinical Child Psychology, 12*, 337–46.

Mattes, J. A., and Gittelman-Klein, R. (1981). Effects of artificial food colorings in children with hyperactive symptoms: A critical review and results of a controlled study. *Archives of General Psychiatry, 38*, 714–18.

McDevitt, S. C. (1990). Attention deficit hyperactivity disorder and treatment. *Early Childhood Update, 6*, 5–7.

McGee, R., Partridge, F., Williams, S., and Silva, P. (1991). A twelve-year follow-up of preschool hyperactive children. *Journal of the American Academy of Child and Adolescent Psychiatry, 30*, 224–32.

McGee, R., Williams, S., and Silva, P. (1984). Background characteristics of aggressive, hyperactive and aggressive-hyperactive boys. *Journal of the American Academy of Child Psychiatry, 23*, 280–84.

McMahon R. C. (1980). Genetic etiology in hyperactive child syndrome: A critical review. *American Journal of Orthopsychiatry, 50*, 145–50.

McMahon, R. C. (1981). Biological factors in childhood hyperkinesis: A review of genetics and biochemical hypothesis. *Journal of Clinical Psychology, 37*, 12–21.

Milich, R, Loney, J., and Landau, S. (1982). Independent dimensions of hyperactivity and aggression: A validation with playroom observation data. *Journal of Abnormal Psychology, 91*, 183–98.

Palmer, S., Rapoport, J. L., and Quinn, P. O. (1975). Food additives and hyperactivity. *Clinical Pediatrics, 14,* 956–59.

Pennington, B. F. (1991). *Diagnosing Learning Disorders.* New York: Guilford Press.

Ralph, J. C. (1991a). Spotting attention deficit disorder. *Pediatric News, 25,* 26.

Ralph, J. C. (1991b). Update on dyslexia. *Pediatric News, 25,* 15.

Rapoport, J., and Buchsbaum, M. (1978). Dextroamphetamine: Cognitive and behavioral effect in normal prepubertal boys. *Science, 199,* 560.

Rapoport, J., Buchsbaum, M., Weingartner, H., Zahn, T., Ludlow, C., and Nickkelsen, E. (1980). Dextroamphetamine: Its cognitive and behavioral effects in normal and hyperactive boys and normal men. *Archives of Journal of Psychiatry, 37,* 933–43.

Rapoport, J., and Ismond, D. (1990). DSM-III-R training guide for diagnosis of childhood disorders. New York: Brunner-Mazel.

Sandberg, S. T., Rutter, M., and Taylor, E. (1978). Hyperkinetic disorder in psychiatry clinic attenders. *Developmental Medicine and Child Neurology, 20,* 279–99.

Satterfield, J. H., Cantwell, D. P., and Satterfield, B. T. (1980). Multimodality treatment: A one-year follow-up of eighty-four hyperactive boys. *Archives of General Psychiatry, 36,* 1965–74.

Shaywitz, S. E., and Shaywitz, B. A. (1991). Introduction to the special series on attention deficit disorder. *Journal of Learning Disabilities, 24,* 68–71.

Shekim, W. O., Dekirmenjian, H., Chapel, J. L, Javaid, J., and Davis, J. M. (1979). Norepinephrine metabolism and clinical response to dextroamphetamine in hyperactive boys. *Journal of Pediatrics, 95,* 389–94.

Simeon, J. G. (1991). Children with conduct disorder may benefit from use of Ritalin. *Pediatric News, 25,* 5.

Sosne, J. (1990). *How to Work with a Hyperactive Child in School.* Portland: Children's Program, 5331 SW Macadam, Suite 210, Portland, OR 97201. (Handouts at workshop on October 12, 1990.)

Sprague, R., and Sleator, B. (1976). Drug and dosages: Implications for learning disabilities. In R. M. Knights and D. J. Bakker (eds.), *The Neuropsychology of Learning Disorders.* Baltimore: University Park Press, 351–66.

Sprague, R., and Sleator, B. (1977). Methylphenidate in hyperkinetic children. *Science, 198,* 1274–76.

Taylor, E. A., Schachar, R., Thorley, G., and Wieselberg, M. (1986). Conduct disorder and hyperactivity: I. Separation of hyperactivity and antisocial conduct in British child psychiatric patients. *British Journal of Psychiatry, 149,* 760–67.

Thomas, A. (1965). Significance of temperamental individuality for school functioning. In J. Hellmuth (ed.), *Learning Disorders,* vol. 3. Seattle: Special Child Publications, 347–56.

Thomas, A., and Chess, S. (1963). *Behavioral Individuality in Early Childhood.* New York: New York University Press.

Thomas, A., and Chess, S. (1977). *Temperament and Development.* New York: Brunner-Mazel.

Thomas, A., and Chess, S. (1980). *Dynamics of Psychological Development.* New York: Brunner-Mazel.

United States National Institutes of Health. (1982). Consensus conference: Defined diets and childhood hyperactivity. *Journal of American Medical Association, 248,* 290–92.

Wender, E. (1986). The food additive–free diet in the treatment of behavior disorders: A review. *Journal of Developmental and Behavioral Pediatrics, 7,* 35–42.

Wender, P. H. (1987). *The Hyperactive Child, Adolescent, and Adult.* New York: Oxford University Press.

Werry, J. (1982). An overview of pediatric psychopharmacology. *Journal of American Academy of Child and Adolescent Psychiatry, 21,* 3–9.

Werry, J. S., Sprague, R. L., and Cohen, N. M. (1975). Conners teacher rating scale for use in drug studies with children—an empirical study. *Journal of Abnormal Child Psychology, 3,* 217–29.

Whalen, C. K., and Henker, B. (1976). Psychostimulants and children: A review and analysis. *Psychological Bulletin, 83,* 1113–30.

Williams, J. I., and Cram, D. M. (1978). Diet in the management of hyperkinesis: A review of the tests of Feingold's hypothesis. *Canadian Psychiatric Association Journal, 23,* 241–48.

Wolraich, M. L. (1977). Stimulant drug therapy in hyperactive children: Research and clinical implications. *Pediatrics, 60,* 512–18.

Zametkin, A. J., Nordahl, T. E, and Gross, M. (1990). Cerebral glucose metabolism in adults with hyperactivity of childhood onset. *New England Journal of Medicine, 323,* 1361–66.

Appendixes

APPENDIX A

Conners Rating Scales

Teacher's Questionnaire

Name of Child _____   Grade _____

Date of Evaluation _____

Please answer all questions. Beside *each* item, indicate the degree of the problem by a check mark (✔).

	0	**1**	**2**	**3**
	Not at all	Just a little	Pretty much	Very much
1. Restless in the "squirmy" sense.				
2. Makes inappropriate noises when he shouldn't.				
3. Demands must be met immediately.				
4. Acts "smart" (impudent or sassy).				
5. Temper outbursts and unpredictable behavior.				
6. Overly sensitive to criticism.				
7. Distractibility or attention span a problem.				
8. Disturbs other children.				
9. Daydreams.				
10. Pouts and sulks.				
11. Mood changes quickly and drastically.				
12. Quarrelsome.				
13. Submissive attitude toward authority.				
14. Restless, always "up and on the go."				
15. Excitable, impulsive.				
16. Excessive demands for teacher's attention.				
17. Appears to be unaccepted by group.				
18. Appears to be easily led by other children.				
19. No sense of fair play.				
20. Appears to lack leadership.				
21. Fails to finish things that he starts.				
22. Childish and immature.				
23. Denies mistakes or blames others.				
24. Does not get along well with other children.				
25. Uncooperative with classmates.				
26. Easily frustrated in efforts.				
27. Uncooperative with teacher.				
28. Difficulty in learning.				

Parents's Questionnaire

Name of Child _____   Date _____

Date of birth _____   Name of parent _____

Age _____ Sex _____

Instructions: Please answer all questions. Beside *each* item below, indicate the degree of the problem with a check mark (✔).

	Not at all	Just a little	Pretty much	Very much
1. Picks at things (nails, fingers, hair, clothing).				
2. Sassy to grown-ups.				
3. Problem with making or keeping friends.				
4. Excitable, impulsive.				
5. Wants to run things.				
6. Sucks or chews (thumb; clothing; blankets).				

	Not at all	Just a little	Pretty much	Very much
7. Cries easily or often.				
8. Carries a chip on his or her shoulder.				
9. Daydreams.				
10. Difficulty in learning.				
11. Restless in the "squirmy" sense.				
12. Fearful (of new situations; new people or places; going to school).				

	Not at all	Just a little	Pretty much	Very much
13. Restless, always up and on the go.				
14. Destructive.				
15. Tells lies or stories that aren't true.				
16. Shy.				
17. Gets into more trouble than others same age.				
18. Speaks differently from others same age (baby talk; stuttering; hard to understand).				

	Not at all	Just a little	Pretty much	Very much
19. Denies mistakes or blames others.				
20. Quarrelsome.				
21. Pouts and sulks.				
22. Steals.				
23. Disobedient or obeys but resentfully.				
24. Worries more than others (about being alone; illness or death).				

	Not at all	Just a little	Pretty much	Very much
25. Fails to finish things.				
26. Feelings easily hurt.				
27. Bullies others.				
28. Unable to stop a repetitive activity.				
29. Cruel.				
30. Childish or immature (wants help he or she shouldn't need; clings; needs constant reassurance).				

31. Distractibility or attention span a problem.				
32. Headaches.				
33. Mood changes quickly and drastically.				
34. Doesn't like or doesn't follow rules or restrictions.				
35. Fights constantly.				
36. Doesn't get along well with brothers or sisters.				

37. Easily frustrated in efforts.				
38. Disturbs other children.				
39. Basically an unhappy child.				
40. Problems with eating (poor appetite; up between bites).				
41. Stomachaches.				
42. Problems with sleep (can't fall asleep; up too early; up in the night).				

43. Other aches and pains.				
44. Vomiting or nausea.				
45. Feels cheated in family circle.				
46. Boasts and brags.				
47. Lets self be pushed around.				
48. Bowel problems (frequently loose, irregular habits; constipation).				

U. S. Department of Education—ADD Policy Clarification*

On September 16, 1991, the U.S. Education Department issued a Policy Memorandum, signed by three Department Assistant Secretaries, expressly recognizing children with Attention Deficit Disorder (ADD/HD) qualify for special education and related services under federal law. The Policy makes clear that children with ADD/HD qualify for special education and related services *solely* on the basis of ADD; when the ADD itself impairs educational performance or learning, under *both* (1) Public Law 94-142, Individuals with Disabilities Act (IDEA) Part B, "other health impaired" statutes and regulations, *and* (2) Section 504 of the 1973 Rehabilitation Act plus its implementating regulations.

Introduction from the Department of Education

There is a growing awareness in the education community that the Attention Deficit Disorder (ADD) and Attention Deficit Hyperactivity Disorder (ADHD) can result in significant learning problems for children with those conditions. While estimates of the prevalence of ADD/HD vary widely, we believe that three to five percent of school-age children may have significant educational problems related to these disorders. Because ADD/HD has broad implications for education as a whole, the Department of Education believes it should clarify State and Local responsibility under Federal law for addressing the needs of children with ADD/HD in the schools. Ensuring that these students are able to reach their fullest potential is an inherent part of the National education goals and AMERICA 2000. The National goals, and the strategy for achieving them, are based on the assumptions that: 1) all children can learn and benefit from their education; and 2) the educational community must work to improve the learning opportunities for all children.

State and Local Education Agencies have an affirmative obligation to evaluate a child who is suspected of having a disability to determine the child's need for special education and related services.

A local school district may not refuse to evaluate the possible need for special education and related services of a child with a prior medical diagnosis of ADD/HD solely by reason of that medical diagnosis. However, a medial diagnosis of ADD/HD alone is not sufficient to render a child eligible for services. A full and individual assessment must be conducted in accordance with State and Federal law before placement or denial of special education.

The laws require that a child's evaluation must be conducted by a multidisciplinary team, including at least one teacher or other specialist with knowledge in the area of suspected disability.

Children with ADD/HD, where the ADD/HD is a chronic or acute health problem resulting in limited alertness, may be considered disabled under Part B solely on the basis of this disorder within the "other health impaired" category in situations where special education and related services are needed because of the ADD/HD.

Children with ADD/HD are also eligible for services under Part B if the children satisfy the criteria applicable to other disability categories. For example, children with ADD/HD are also eligible for services under the "specific learning disability" category, or under the category of "seriously emotionally disturbed," if they meet the additional criteria of either of those categories.

Even if a child is determined not to be eligible for special education he/she may be eligible for services under the Federal Law—Rehabilitation Act of 1973 (Section 504), which is designed to prevent discrimination of individuals with disabilities.

IDEA (Individuals with Disabilities Education Act) and Section 504 require adaptions of regular education and/or modification of nonacademic times such as lunchroom, recess and physical education as needed by the student. Both laws require the Local Education Agency to make available a system of procedural safeguards that permits parents to challenge actions regarding the identification, evaluation, or

educational placement of a handicapped child whom they believe needs
special education or related services.

Notice from C.H.A.D.D. Legal Counsel

The Policy contains several key aspects of *immediate* applicability to
children with ADD/HD, in that it:

- *Recognizes ADD/HD as an IDEA Part B "other health impaired"
  disability requiring free special education and related services* specifically designed for ADD/HD needs, *when* the ADD/HD 1) is
  identified through Part B evaluation criteria; 2) is a chronic or
  acute health problem limiting alertness (attention); and 3) ad-
  versely affects education performance.
- *Distinguished ADD/HD from other Part B disabilities* such as
  specific learning disabilities or seriously emotionally disturbed,
  while restating the current legal requirement that children with
  both ADD/HD and any other Part B disability receive appropriate education and services to meet the needs of *each* such
  disability.
- Specifies *both* Part B *rights* of children with ADD/HD to *school
  evaluations* for suspected disabilities and Part B *parent due process
  rights* in case of disagreement over such evaluations.
- *Defines the rights of children with ADD/HD to Section 504 special
  education programs and services* specifically designed for ADD/
  HD education needs, even where such children may not meet
  IDEA Part B criteria.
- Explains Section 504 *regular education classroom adaptation re-
  quirements* for children with ADD/HD who might not need special education and related services.
- *Recommends techniques and methods for successfully educating
  children with ADD/HD* to meet compliance obligations to such
  children.
- Describes ways *the Department will inform, through education
  information centers and other means,* parents, educators and other
  interested persons about how schools should identify, evaluate
  and teach children with ADD/HD.

What Parents and Educators Should Do Now

Parents and educators of children with ADD/HD should consider the following steps to assure effective implementation of the Department ADD/HD Policy for the children's benefits:

- Inform their own school/school district administrators and special educators about this Policy *now*.
- Determine what school and school districts *are already doing* to educate ADD/HD children effectively, and assess how the Policy will bolster such efforts.
- Encourage special and regular educators to seek ADD/HD in-service training opportunities and get familiar with how to educate children with ADD/HD more effectively.
- See *immediate, voluntary* implementation of this Policy in state education regulations and policies, by joining other parents, health professionals and educators in forming state ADD/HD Councils to advocate such steps.
- Work with state legislators to get *more state funds* for special education plus ADD/HD pre-service and in-service educator training, also through state ADD/HD Councils.
- Help *other parents and educators* of children with ADD/HD learn about and understand this important Policy now.

APPENDIX C
ADHD Clinics

The following is a partial list of programs that serve ADHD children with team evaluations. Budgetary cutbacks can put any clinic out of business quickly, so please call your local clinic for current information.

Arkansas

University Hospital and Ambulatory Care Center
4310 W. Markham St.
Little Rock, AR 72205

California

Mental Retardation and Developmental Disabilities Program

University of California at Los Angeles
300 Medical Plaza
Los Angeles, CA 90024

District of Columbia

Georgetown University Hospital, Child Development Center

Dir.—Elliot Gersh, M.D.
Georgetown University–Child Development Center
3800 Reservoir Road, N.W.
Washington, D.C. 20007

Delaware

Alfred I. Dupont Institute
1600 Rockland Rd.
P.O. Box 269
Wilmington, Delaware 19899

Florida

University of South Florida College of Medicine

Dir.—D. Karnister, M.D.
University of South Florida
F.M.H.I. Building C, Room 7-221
13301 N. 30th Street
Tampa, FL 33612

Maryland

John F. Kennedy Institute for Handicapped Children, Johns Hopkins Hospital

Dir.—Arnold J. Capute, M.D.
The John F. Kennedy Institute for Handicapped Children
707 N. Broadway
Baltimore, MD 21205

University of Maryland

Dir.—Murray M. Kappelman, M.D.
Division of Behavioral and Developmental Pediatrics
University of Maryland
Walter P. Carter, Room 5-670
UMAB Campus
Baltimore, MD 21201

Massachusetts

Children's Hospital

Dir.—Eli H. Newberger, M.D.
Children's Hospital
300 Longwood Avenue
Boston, MA 02115

University of Massachusetts Medical School

Russell Barkley, Ph.D.
Dept. of Psychiatry
U. of Massachusetts Medical School
55 Lake Ave. N.
Worcester, MA 01655

Schriver Center
200 Trapelo Rd.
Waltham, MA 02254

Dr. Peter Rosenberg
Massachusetts General Hospital
32 Fruit St.
Boston, MA 02114

Michigan

Mt. Carmel Mercy Hospital

Dir.—John M. Turnbow, M.D.
6071 West Outer Drive
Detroit, MI 48235

Missouri

Knights of Columbus
Developmental Center
Cardinal Glennon Children's
Hospital
1465 South Grand Blvd.
St. Louis, Missouri 63104-1095

New York

Albert Einstein College of Medicine, Montefiore Medical Center

Department of Pediatrics
Montifiore Medical Center
118 E 210th Street
Bronx, NY 10467

North Shore University Hospital Cornell University College of Medicine

Dir.—David Meryash, M.D., Chief
Department of Pediatrics
Child Development Center
North Shore University Hospital
300 Community Drive
Manhasset, NY 11030

University of Rochester Medical Center

Dir.—S. B. Sulkes, M.D.
University of Rochester Medical
Center
601 Elmwood Avenue, Box 671
Rochester, NY 14642

C. Keith Connors, Ph.D.
Multi-Health Systems Inc.
908 Niagara Falls Blvd.
North Tonawanda, NY 14120-2060

Genesee Hospital
224 Alexander
Rochester, NY 14607

SUNY Health Sciences Center at
Syracuse (University Hospital)
750 E. Adams
Syracuse, NY 13210

North Carolina

Melvin D. Levine, M.D.
Clinical Center for the Study of Development and Learning
CB # 7255, BSRC
University of North Carolina
Chapel Hill, NC 27599-7255

Oklahoma

Richard Wansley, Ph.D.
Child Development Program
Oklahoma State University-College
of Osteopathic Medicine
1111 West 7th
Tulsa, OK 74107

Oregon

Child Development and Rehabilitation Center,
Oregon Health Sciences University

Dir.—G. Sells, M.D.
Child Development and Rehabilitation Center
P.O. Box 574
(707 SW Gaines)
Portland, OR 97207

The Children's Program
The Water Tower at John's Landing
5331 SW Macadam Ave. Suite 210
Portland, OR 97201

Oregon Health Sciences University
(C.D.R.C. - Eugene)
Clinical Services Bldg.
901 E. 18th Ave.
Eugene, OR 97403-1303

Emanual Hospital Medical Center
Dr. S. Budden
2801 N. Gantenbein Ave.
Portland, OR 97227

Pennsylvania

Children's Hospital of Philadelphia/
University of Pennsylvania

Dir.—Henry S. Cecil, M.D.
Division of Child Development and
Rehabilitation
Room 2307
The Children's Hospital of
Philadelphia
3400 Civic Center Boulevard
Philadelphia, PA 19104

Children's Hospital of Pittsburgh/
University of Pittsburgh School of
Medicine

Dir.—Heidi Feldman, M.D.
Child Development Unit
Children's Hospital of Pittsburgh
125 DeSoto Street
Pittsburgh, PA 14213

St. Christopher's Hospital for
Children
Fifth & Lehigh Ave.
Philadelphia, PA 19133

Thomas Jefferson University
Hospital
11th & Walnuts Sts.
Philadelphia, PA 19107

Hospital of the Medical College of
Pennsylvania
(formerly Eastern Pennsylvania Psychiatric Institute)
3300 Henry Ave.
Philadelphia, PA 19129

Rhode Island

*Rhode Island Hospital/Brown
University*

Dir.—S. M. Pueschel, M.D.
Child Development Center
Rhode Island Hospital
593 Eddy Street
Providence, RI 02902

Tennessee

School Performance Clinic
Child Development Center
Vanderbilt University Medical
Center
426 Medical Center South
Nashville, TN 37232-3573

*University of Tennessee Center for
Health Sciences
Child Development Center*

Dir.—M. E. Soto-Viera, M.D.
711 Jefferson Avenue
Memphis, TN 38105

Texas

*University of Texas Medical Branch,
Galveston*

Dir.—Bobbye M. Rouse, M.D.
Child Health Center
UTMB Hospitals, Pediatric
Department
Galveston, TX 77550

*William Beaumont Army Medical
Center*

Dir.—A. W. Atkinson, M.D.
Developmental Pediatrics Services
WBAMC
El Paso, TX 79920

Charles Ginsberg, M.D.
Clinical Services Coordinator
University Affiliated Plaza Exchange
Park
Dallas, TX 75235

Baylor University Medical Center
3500 Gaston Ave.
Dallas, TX 75246

Texas Children's Hospital
6621 Fannin St.
Houston, TX 77030

Washington

Madigan Army Medical Center

Dir.—Dr. Kelly
Child Development Fellowship
Program
Box 870
Madigan Army Medical Center
Tacoma, WA 98431

Colleges with Learning Disorder Services

The following information was taken from *Peterson's Guide to Colleges with Programs for Learning-Disabled Students,* 2d ed. (Princeton, NJ: Peterson's Guides, 1988). The guide was edited by Charles T. Mangrum II, Ed. D., and Stephen S. Strichart. Schools marked with bold letters are listed as providing learning-disorder programs. Those not in bold letters have services for students with learning disorders.

Alabama

Alabama Aviation and Technical College
Auburn University at Montgomery
Chattahoochee Valley State Community College
George Corley Wallace State Community College, Selma
Troy State University at Dothan
University of Alabama, Tuscaloosa
University of Alabama at Birmingham
University of Montevallo
University of South Alabama

Alaska

University of Alaska, Anchorage
University of Alaska, Fairbanks

Arizona

Arizona State University
Eastern Arizona College

Glendale Community College
Grand Canyon College
Mesa Community College
Northern Arizona University
Phoenix College
Pima Community College
Scottsdale Community College
South Mountain Community College

Arkansas

Arkansas State University
Harding University
Mississippi County Community College
Southern Arkansas University, Fayetteville
University of Arkansas, Fayetteville
University of the Ozarks

California

Allan Hancock College
Antelope Valley College

Bakerfield College
Barstow College
Biola University
Butte College
California Lutheran University
California Polytechnic State University, San Luis Obispo
California State Polytechnic University, Pomona
California State University, Bakerfield
California State University, Chico
California State University, Dominquez Hills
California State University, Fullerton
California State University, Hayward
California State University, Northridge
California State University, Sacramento
California State University, San Bernardino
California State University, Stanislaus
Cañada College
Cerritos College
Chapman College
Christ College Irvine
Coastline Community College
College of Alameda
College of the Canyons
College of the Desert
College of the Sequoias
Columbia College, Columbia
Contra Costa College
Cosumnes River College
Crafton Hills College
Cuesta College
Cypress College
De Anza College
East Los Angeles College
El Camino College

Evergreen Valley College
Feather River College
Foothill College
Fresno City College
Fullerton College
Hartnell College
Holy Names College
Humboldt State University
Imperial Valley College
Irvine Valley College
King's River Community College
Laney College
Long Beach City College
Los Angeles City College
Los Angeles Mission College
Los Angeles Valley College
Marin Community College
Merritt College
Mira Costa College
Modesto Junior College
Monterey Peninsula College
Mt. San Antonio College
Mt. San Jacinto College
Napa Valley College
Ohlone College
Orange Coast College
Oxnard College
Porterville College
Rancho Santiago College
San Diego City College
San Diego Mesa College
San Diego State University
San Francisco State University
Santa Barbara City College
Santa Monica College
Santa Rosa Junior College
Scripps College
Shasta College
Sierra College
Skyline College
Solano Community College
Sonoma State University
Southwestern College
Stanford University

Taft College
University of California, Berkeley
University of California, Davis
University of California, Irvine
University of California, Los
  Angeles
University of California, Riverside
University of California, Santa
  Barbara
University of California, Santa Cruz
University of Redlands
University of Southern California
Ventura College
Victor Valley College
West Hills College
West Valley College

Colorado

Arapahoe Community College
Colorado Northwestern Commu-
  nity College
Colorado State University
Community College of Aurora
Community College of Denver
Fort Lewis College
Front Range Community College
Lamar Community College
Northeastern Junior College
Pikes Peak Community College
Red Rocks Community College
Regis College
Trinidad State Junior College
University of Colorado at Boulder
University of Denver
University of Southern Colorado

Connecticut

Hartford College for Women
Housatonic Community College
Mattatuck Community College
Mitchell College
Northwestern Connecticut Commu-
  nity College

Norwalk Community College
Sacred Heart University
South Central Community College
Southern Connecticut State
  University
Thames Valley State Technical
  College
Trinity College
University of Connecticut, Storrs
Western Connecticut State
  University

Delaware

Brandywine College of Widener
  University
Delaware Technical and Community
  College, Terry Campus

District of Columbia

American University
George Washington University
Howard University

Florida

Baptist Bible Institute
Edison Community College
Embry-Riddle Aeronautical
  University
Florida Agriculture and Mechani-
  cal University
Florida Atlantic University
Florida Community College at
  Jacksonville
Florida International University
Florida State University
Gulf Coast Community College
Indian River Community College
Lake City Community College
Miami-Dade Community College
Okaloosa-Walton Junior College
Palm Beach Atlantic College
Pensacola Junior College

Polk Community College
St. Johns River Community College
Santa Fe Community College
Seminole Community College
Tallahassee Community College
University of Florida
University of North Florida
University of Tampa
University of West Florida
Valencia Community College

Georgia

Berry College
Brenau Women's College
Clayton State College
DeVry Institute of Technology
East Georgia College
Emory University
Georgia College
Georgia Institute of Technology
Georgia Southern College
Georgia State University
Mercer University, Macon
Mercer University, Atlanta
Paine College
Piedmont College
Southern College of Technology
South Georgia College
University of Georgia
West Georgia College

Guam

University of Guam

Hawaii

Brigham Young University—Hawaii
University of Hawaii at Manoa
University of Hawaii—Honolulu
   Community College
University of Hawaii—Kapiolani
   Community College

University of Hawaii—Kauai Community College
**University of Hawaii—Leeward
Community College**

Idaho

Boise State University
North Idaho College
University of Idaho

Illinois

Aurora University
Barat College
Chicago State University
City Colleges of Chicago, Chicago
   City-Wide College
Danville Area Community College
De Paul University
Elgin Community College
Felician College
Governors State University
Highland Community College
Illinois Central College
Illinois Eastern Community Colleges, Frontier Community
   College
Illinois Eastern Community Colleges, Lincoln Trail College
Illinois Eastern Community Colleges, Olney Central College
Illinois Eastern Community Colleges, Wabash Valley College
Illinois State University
Illinois Technical College
John A. Logan College
John Wood Community College
Kendall College
Kishwaukee College
Knox College
Lake Land College
Lewis and Clark Community
   College

Lincoln College
Lincoln Land Community College
Moraine Valley Community College
Morton College
Mundelein College
National College of Education
Northeastern Illinois University
Northern Illinois University
Oakton Community College
Parkland College
Richland Community College
Roosevelt University
Rosary College
School of the Art Institute of Chicago
Shawnee College
Shimer College
Southeastern Illinois College
Southern Illinois University at Carbondale
Southern Illinois University at Edwardsville
University of Illinois at Urbana-Champaign
Waubonsee Community College
Western Illinois University
William Rainey Harper College

Indiana

Ancilla Domini College
Anderson College
Goshen College
Indiana Institute of Technology
Indiana State University
Indiana University Bloomington
Indiana University East
Indiana University Northwest
Indiana University—Purdue University at Indianapolis
Indiana Vocational Technical College—Central Indiana

Indiana Vocational Technical College—Eastcentral
Indiana Vocational Technical College—Kokomo
Indiana Vocational Technical College—Northcentral
Indiana Vocational Technical College—Northeast
Indiana Vocational Technical College—Southcentral
Indiana Vocational Technical College—Southeast
Indiana Vocational Technical College—Whitewater
Indiana Wesleyan University
Martin Center College
Purdue University, West Lafayette
Saint Joseph's College
University of Evansville
University of Southern Indiana

Iowa

Clinton Community College
Coe College
Cornell College
Graceland College
Grand View College
Hawkeye Institute of Technology
Indian Hills Community College
Iowa Central Community College
Iowa Lakes Community College, North Attendance Center
Iowa Lakes Community College, South Attendance Center
Iowa State University
Iowa Wesleyan College
Iowa Western Community College
Loras College
Luther College
Morningside College
Muscatine Community College
National Education Center, Na-

tional Institute of Technology
Campus
North Iowa Area Community
College
Northwestern College
Scott Community College
Southeastern Community College,
North Campus
Southwestern Community College
University of Iowa

Kansas

**Butler County Community
College**
Cowley County Community
College
Emporia State University
Fort Scott Community College
Friends Bible College
Highland Community College
Hutchinson Community College
Kansas City Kansas Community
College
Kansas Newman College
Kansas State University
Pittsburg State University
Wichita State University

Kentucky

Brescia College
Eastern Kentucky University
Lindsey Wilson College
Northern Kentucky University
Paducah Community College
Thomas More College
University of Kentucky, Lexington
Community College
University of Louisville

Maine

Bates College
Bowdoin College

Eastern Maine Vocational Technical
College Institute
Mid-State College
Southern Maine Vocational Techni-
cal Institute
Unity College
University of Maine at Orono
University of Maine at Fort Kent
University of Maine at Machias
University of New England

Maryland

Catonsville Community College
Charles County Community
College
Chesapeake College
Columbia Union College
Community College of Baltimore
Frostburg State University
Hagerstown Junior College
Howard Community College
Johns Hopkins University
**Montgomery College, German-
town Campus**
Prince George's Community
College
Towson State University
University of Maryland Baltimore
County
University of Maryland Eastern
Shore
Western Maryland College

Massachusetts

American International College
Amherst College
Anna Maria College for Men and
Women
Aquinas Junior College, Newton
Bentley College
Boston College
Boston University
Bradford College

Bridgewater State College
Bristol Community College
Cape Cod Community College
Clark University
Curry College
Eastern Nazarene College
Endicott College
Essex Agricultural and Technical
Institute
Framingham State College
Harvard University
**Massachsuetts Bay Community
College**
Massasoit Community College
Middlesex Community College
Mount Ida College
Mount Wachusett Community
College
Newbury College
Northeastern University
Northern Essex Community
College
North Shore Community College
Pine Manor College
Simmons College
Smith College
Southeastern Massachusetts
University
Springfield Technical Community
College
Stonehill College
Suffolk University
Tufts University
University of Lowell
University of Massachusetts at
Amherst
**University of Massachusetts at
Boston**
Wellesley College
Wheaton College

Michigan

Adrian College
Alma College
Aquinas College
Center for Creative Studies—Col-
lege of Arts and Design
Central Michigan University
Charles Stewart Mott Community
College
Delta College
Detroit College of Business,
Dearborn
Detroit College of Business, Madi-
son Heights Campus
Glen Oaks Community College
Grand Rapids Junior College
Henry Ford Community College
Hope College
Jackson Community College
Lake Michigan College
Lake Superior State University
Lansing Community College
Mercy College of Detroit
Michigan Technological University
Mid Michigan Community College
Monroe County Community
College
Montcalm Community College
Northern Michigan University
Northwestern Michigan College
Oakland Community College
Oakland University
St. Clair County Community
College
Schoolcraft College
University of Michigan, Ann Arbor
Washtenaw Community College
Western Michigan University

Minnesota

Alexandria Technical Institute
**Anoka-Ramey Community
College**

Augsburg College
Austin Community College
Bemidji State University
Bethel College
College of St. Catherine
College of St. Scholastica
Fergus Falls Community College
Hibbing Community College
Inver Hills Community College
Itasca Community College
Lakewood Community College
Lowthian College
Mesabi Community College
Minneapolis Community College
Moorhead State University
North Hennepin Community
 College
Rochester Community College
St. Cloud State University
Saint John's University
St. Olaf College
University of Minnesota, Duluth
University of Minnesota, Morris
University of Minnesota, Technical
 College, Crookston
**University of Minnesota, Twin
 Cities Campus**
Willmar Community College
Worthington Community College

Mississippi

Hinds Community College
University of Mississippi
William Carey College

Missouri

Central Methodist State University
East Central College
Evangel College
Jefferson College
Kansas City Art Institute
Lindenwood College

Maple Woods Community College
Missouri Southern State College
Northwest Missouri State College
Rockhurst College
Saint Louis Community College at
 Florissant Valley
Saint Louis Community College at
 Forest Park
Southwest Missouri State University
University of Missouri—Columbus
University of Missouri—Rolla
Washington University
Webster University
Westminster College

Montana

Dull Knife Memorial College
Flathead Valley Community College
Montana State University
Northern Montana College
Western Montana College

Nebraska

Central Community College, Grand
 Island Campus
Concordia Teachers College
Dana College
Hastings College
Southeast Community College, Bea-
 trice Campus
Union College
University of Nebraska—Lincoln
Wayne State College
Western Nebraska Community Col-
 lege, Scottsbluff Campus

Nevada

Truckee Meadows Community
 College
University of Nevada—Reno

New Hampshire

Dartmouth College
Franklin Pierce College
Hesser College
Keene State College
New England College
New Hampshire College
New Hampshire Vocational-Technical College, Laconia
New Hampshire Vocational-Technical College, Stratham
University of New Hampshire, Durham
White Pines College

New Jersey

Caldwell College
College of Saint Elizabeth
Fairleigh Dickinson University, Teaneck-Hackensack Campus
Georgian Court College
Gloucester County College
Hudson County Community College
New Jersey Institute of Technology
Ocean County College
Princeton University
Rutgers, The State University of New Jersey, Rutgers College
Stockton State College
Trenton State College
Upsala College
William Paterson College of New Jersey

New Mexico

New Mexico Institute of Mining and Technology
New Mexico Junior College
Northern New Mexico Community College

Santa Fe College
University of New Mexico, Valencia Branch
Western New Mexico University

New York

Adelphi University
Broome Community College
Canisius College
Cazenovia College
City College of the City University of New York
College of New Rochelle, New Resources Division
College of Staten Island of the City University of New York
Columbia-Greene Community College
Community College of the Finger Lakes
Cornell University
Dutchess Community College
Elizabeth Seton College
Fashion Institute of Technology
Fiorello H. LaGuardia Community College of the City University of New York
Fulton-Montgomery Community College
Genesee Community College
Herkimer County Community College
Hofstra University
Houghton College
Hudson Valley Community College
Hunter College of the City University of New York
Jamestown Community College
Jefferson Community College
John Jay College of Criminal Justice of the City University of New York

Manhattan College
Marist College
Medaille College
Mercy College
Mohawk Valley Community
College
Nassau Community College
New York City Technical College
of the City University of New
York
New York University
Niagara County Community
College
Niagara University
Onondaga Community College
Orange County Community
College
Paul Smith's College
Polytechnic University, Farmingdale
Campus
Queensborough Community College of the City University of
New York
Queens College of the City University of New York
Rensselaer Polytechnic Institute
Rochester Institute of Technology
Rockland Community College
St. Thomas Aquinas College
Schenectady County Community
College
State University of New York at
Albany
State University of New York at
Binghamton
State University of New York at
Buffalo
**State University of New York at
Stony Brook**
State University of New York College at Brockport
State University of New York College at Buffalo

State University of New York College at Fredonia
State University of New York College at Oneonta
State University of New York College at Plattsburgh
State University of New York College at Potsdam
State University of New York College at Purchase
State University of New York College of Agriculture and Technology at Cobleskill
State University of New York College of Agriculture and Technology at Morrisville
State University of New York College of Environmental Science and Forestry
State University of New York College of Technology at Alfred
State University of New York College of Technology at Canton
State University of New York College of Technology at Delhi
State University of New York College of Technology at Farmingdale
State University of New York College of Technology at Utica/Rome
Suffolk County Community College, Ammerman Campus
Suffolk County Community College, Western Campus
Syracuse University
Ulster County Community College
Utica College of Syracuse University
Vassar College
Villa Maria College of Buffalo
Westchester Community College

North Carolina

Anson Community College
Appalachian State University
Caldwell Community College and
    Technical Institute
Catawba Valley Community
    College
Central Piedmont Community
    College
Chowan College
Craven Community College
Davidson County Community
    College
East Carolina University
Forsyth Technical Community
    College
Guilford Technical Community
    College
Isothermal Community College
Mars Hill College
McDowell Technical Community
    College
North Carolina State University
    at Raleigh
North Carolina Wesleyan College
Pitt Community College
Randolph Community College
Rockingham Community College
Saint Mary's College
Sampson Community College
Sandhills Community College
Southwestern Community College
Tri-County Community College
University of North Carolina at
    Chapel Hill
University of North Carolina at
    Charlotte
University of North Carolina at
    Greensboro
University of North Carolina at
    Wilmington
Wake Forest University
Western Carolina University

Wilkes Community College
Wilson County Technical College
Wingate College

North Dakota

Bismarck State College
Mayville State University
North Dakota State College of
    Science
North Dakota State University
North Dakota State University—
    Bottineau Branch and Institute of
    Forestry

Ohio

Bowling Green State University
Case Western Reserve University
Central Ohio Technical College
Cincinnati Technical College
Cleveland Institute of Art
College of Mount St. Joseph
Columbus State Community
    College
Cuyahoga Community College,
    Eastern Campus
Cuyahoga Community College,
    Western Campus
Defiance College
Denison University
Edison State Community College
Findlay College
Franklin University
Hiram College
Hocking Technical College
Jefferson Technical College
Malone College
Marion Technical College
Miami University Middletown
    Campus
Muskingum College
Northwest Technical College
Notre Dame College of Ohio
Oberlin College

Ohio State University Agricultural
Technical Institute
Ohio State University, Marion
Campus
Ohio State University, Columbus
Campus
Ohio University, Athens
Otterbein College
Owens Technical College
Sinclair Community College
Southern Ohio College, Fairfield
Campus
Southern Ohio College, Northeast
Campus
Southern State Community College
University of Cincinnati
University of Cincinnati, Raymond
Walters General and Technical
College
University of Dayton
University of Toledo
Walsh College
Wilmington College of Ohio
Wright State University

Oklahoma

Cameron University
Carl Albert Junior College
East Central Oklahoma State
University
Oklahoma City Community
College
Oklahoma State University
Oklahoma State University Techni-
cal Branch, Oklahoma City
Oklahoma State University Techni-
cal Branch, Okmulgee
Rose State College
Tulsa Junior College
University of Oklahoma

Oregon

Clackamas Community College
Columbia Christian College
George Fox College
Lane Community College
Linn-Benton Community College
Mt. Hood Community College
Oregon State University
Portland State University
Reed College
Rogue Community College
Southern Oregon State College
Southwestern Oregon Community
College
Umpqua Community College
Western Oregon State College

Pennsylvania

Albright College
Bryn Mawr College
**California University of
Pennsylvania**
Chestnut Hill College
College Mesericordia
**Community College of Allegheny
County, Allegheny Campus**
Community College of Allegheny
County, Boyce Campus
Community College of Allegheny
County, College Center—North
Community College of
Pennsylvania
Delaware County Community
College
Delaware Valley College of Science
and Agriculture
Drexel University
**Edinboro University of
Pennsylvania**
Geneva College
Gettysburg College
Gwynedd-Mercy College
Indiana University of Pennsylvania

Kutztown University of
    Pennsylvania
Lehigh County Community College
Lock Haven University of
    Pennsylvania
Luzerne County Community
    College
Lycoming College
Manor Junior College
Mansfield University of
    Pennsylvania
Mercyhurst College
Northhampton County Area
    Community College
Peirce Junior College
Pennsylvania Institute of
    Technology
Pennsylvania State University, Mont
    Alto Campus
Pennsylvania State University, Park
    Campus
Pennsylvanis State University,
    Schuylkill Campus
Pennsylvania State University,
    Shenango Valley Campus
Pennsylvania State University, Wor-
    thington Scranton Campus
Philadelphia College of Bible
Reading Area Community College
Robert Morris College
Saint Francis College
Spring Garden College
Thaddeus Stevens State School of
    Technology
University of Pennsylvania
University of Pittsburgh, Pittsburgh
University of Pittsburgh, Bradford
University of the Arts
Villa Maria College
Waynesburg College
Westmoreland County Community
    College
Widener University, Pennsylvania
    Campus

Williamsport Area Community
    College

Puerto Rico

American University of Puerto Rico
Caribbean University College
Puerto Rico Junior College
University of Puerto Rico,
    Aguadialla Regional College
University of Puerto Rico, Arecibo
    Technological University College
University of Puerto Rico. Maya-
    güez Campus
University of Puerto Rico, Río
    Piedras

Rhode Island

Bryant College
Community College of Rhode Is-
    land, Knight Campus
Johnson and Wales College
Rhode Island College
University of Rhode Island

South Carolina

Beaufort Technical College
The Citadel, The Military College
    of South Carolina
Coastal Carolina College, Univer-
    sity of South Carolina
College of Charleston
Francis Marion College
Lander College
Midlands Technical College
North Greenville College
Trident Technical College
University of South Carolina,
    Columbia
University of South Carolina at
    Aiken

South Dakota

Black Hills State College
Huron College
National College

Tennessee

Austin Peay State University
Bryan College
Lee College
Memphis State College
Middle Tennessee State University
State Technical Institute at Memphis
Tomlinson College
Tusculum College
**University of Tennessee at
Chattanooga**
University of Tennessee at
Knoxville
Vanderbilt University

Texas

Amarillo College
Angelina College
Brookhaven College
Cisco Junior College
College of the Mainland
Eastfield College
East Texas Baptist University
El Paso, County Community
College
Hill Junior College
Houston Community College
System
Lamar University
Lamar University—Port Arthur
Laredo Junior College
North Harris County College
Northlake College
Pan American University
Richland College
St. Edward's University
St. Mary's University of San
Antonio

San Antonio College
San Jacinto College, Central
Campus
San Jacinto College, South Campus
Schreiner College
Southern Methodist University
Southwestern Junior College of the
Assemblies of God
Southwest Texas State University
Sul Ross State University
Texas A&I University
Texas A&M University, College
Station
Texas Southmost College
Texas State Technical Institute,
Sweetwater Campus
Texas Woman's University
Tyler Junior College
University of North Texas
University of Texas at Dallas
University of Texas at El Paso
University of Texas at San Antonio
West Texas State University

Utah

Brigham Young University
Latter-day Saints Business College
Salt Lake Community College
Snow College
Southern Utah State College
University of Utah
Utah State University
Westminster College of Salt Lake
City

Vermont

Burlington College
Community College of Vermont
Landmark College
Norwich University
Southern Vermont College
University of Vermont
Vermont Technical College

Virginia

Blue Ridge Community College
College of William and Mary
Commonwealth College, Virginia
    Beach
Emory & Henry College
Ferrum College
George Mason University
Hampden-Sydney College
James Madison Community College
John Tyler Community College
Liberty University
Lord Fairfax Community College
New River Community College
Old Dominion University
Patrick Henry Community College
Paul D. Camp Community College
Radford University
Randolph-Macon Woman's College
Rappahannock Community College
Southern Seminary College
Southwest Virginia Community
    College
Thomas Nelson Community
    College
Tidewater College, Chesapeake
    Campus
Tidewater Community College,
    Portsmouth Campus
Tidewater Community College,
    Virginia Beach Campus
University of Virginia
Virginia Intermont College
Virginia Polytechnic Institute and
    State University
Virginia Western Community
    College

Washington

Centralia College
Central Washington University
Clark College
Eastern Washington University
Edmonds Community College
Evergreen State College, The
Highline Community College
North Seattle Community College
Olympic College
South Puget Sound Community
    College
South Seattle Community College
Spokane Community College
Spokane Falls Community College
University of Washington
Western Washington University
Whitworth College

West Virginia

Bethany College
Bluefield State College
Davis & Elkins College
Fairmont State College
Marshall University
Parkersburg Community College
Salem College
Southern West Virginia Community
    College
West Virginia Northern Community
    College
West Virginia State College
West Virginia University
West Virginia Wesleyan College
Wheeling Jesuit College

Wisconsin

Blackhawk Technical College
Carthage College
Chippewa Valley Technical College
Edgewood College
Fox Valley Technical College
Gateway Technical College
Lawrence University
Marian College of Fond du Lac
Marquette University
Mid-State Technical College
Milwaukee Area Technical College

North Central Technical College
Northeast Wisconsin Technical
    College
Ripon College
University of Wisconsin—La
    Crosse
University of Wisconsin—Madison
**University of Wisconsin—
    Milwaukee**
University of Wisconsin—Oshkosh
University of Wisconsin—Platteville
University of Wisconsin—River
    Falls
**University of Wisconsin—
    Whitewater**
University of Wisconsin Center—
    Rock County

University of Wisconsin Center—
    Waukesha County
**Waukesha County Technical
    College**
Western Wisconsin Technical
    College
Wisconsin Indianhead Technical
    College, Ashland Campus

Wyoming

Laramie County Community
    College
Sheridan College
University of Wyoming

APPENDIX E
Parent Support Associations for ADHD

A large number of parent support groups for individuals with ADHD exist in North America. The addresses below are intended to help facilitate your search for a local support group. If you contact CHADD or ADDA, they will give the name and address of the support group nearest you.

Children with Attention Deficit Disorder (CHADD)
National Headquarters
499 NW 70th Ave
Suite 308
Plantation, FL 33322

Attention Deficit Disorder Association (ADDA)
4300 West Park Boulevard
Plano, TX 75093

Learning Disabilities Associations provide information on all learning disorders, not just ADHD.

Learning Disabilities Association of America
4156 Library Road
Pittsburgh, PA 15234

A national newsletter on ADHD can be obtained from this address:

Challenge
A Newsletter on Attention-Deficit Hyperactivity Disorder

P.O. Box 2110
West Newbury, MA 01985

Other support associations are as follows:

Alabama

Hyperspace
3603 Eighth Avenue
Birmingham, AL 35222
(205) 328-1717

Arizona

Arizona Council on Behalf of Children and Adults with Attention Deficit Disorders
3881 West Sunny Shadows
Tucson, AZ 85741

Arkansas

Learning Disabilities Association of Arkansas
P.O. Box 7316
Little Rock, AR 72216
(501) 666-8777

California

California Association for Children
and Adults with Learning
Disorders
17 Buena Vista Avenue
Mill Valley, CA 94941
(415) 383-5242

Colorado

Attention Deficit Disorders Advo-
cacy Group
8091 South Ireland Way
Aurora, CO 80016
(303) 690-7548

Colorado Association for Children
and Adults with Learning
Disabilities
1045 Lincoln St., #106
Denver, CO 80203

Delaware

New Castle County Association for
Children and Adults with Learn-
ing Disabilities
P.O. Box 577
Bear, DE 19701

Florida

ADD-UP
392 Glenbrook Drive
Lantana, FL 33462

PARADE, Inc.
P.O. Box 2569
Orlando, FL 32802-2569

Georgia

ADD Support Group of Columbus
P.O. Box 7412
Columbus, GA 31908-7412

Hawaii

Hawaii Association for Children and
Adults with Learning Disabilities
Room 103
200 North Vineyard
Honolulu, HI 96817

Idaho

ADD Support Group
8420 Holbrook Court
Boise, ID 83704

It All ADDS UP
Pocatello Chapter
5174 Redfish
Chubbick, ID 83202

Illinois

Children with Attention Deficit
Disorders
North Suburban Branch
P.O. Box 99
Winnetka, IL 60093

Iowa

Attention Deficit Disorder—Understanding Parents (ADD—UP)
3034 Sweetbriar
Iowa City, IA 52242
(319) 351-2520

Support Group for Parents of Children with ADD
5114 Gordon Avenue, N.W.
Cedar Rapids, IA 52405
(319) 396-5239

Kansas

Kansas Association for Children and
Adults with Learning Disabilities
P.O. Box 4424
Topeka, KS 66604
(913) 234-9336

Kentucky

ADD Parent Support Group
c/o Our Lady of Peace Hospital
2020 Newbury Road
Louisville, KY 40232
(502) 896-2612

Maine

Special Needs Parent Information
  Network
P.O. Box 2067
Augusta, ME 04330
1-800-325-0220

Maryland

Attention Deficit Disorder Support
  Group of Howard County
9222 Mellenbrook Road
Columbia, MD 21045
(301) 992-7550

Massachusetts

ADD Parent Support Group
  Network
47 Kristin Road
Plymouth, MA 02360
(508) 746-3959

New England Attention Disorders
  Support Group (NEAD)
P.O. Box 82
Northborough, MA 01532
(508) 393-8039

Michigan

ADD Association of Michigan
P.O. Box 9037
Livonia, MI 48154
(313) 464-8233

Minnesota

Co-ADD
The Coalition for Education and
  Support of ADD
P.O. Box 242
Osseo, MN 55369-0242
(612) 493-3177

Minnesota Association for Children
  and Adults with Learning
  Disabilities
#494-N
1821 University Ave.
St. Paul, MN 55104
(612) 646-6136

Mississippi

Mississippi Association for Children
  and Adults with Learning
  Disabilities
P.O. Box 9387
Jackson, MS 39206
(601) 982-2812

Missouri

Missouri Association for Children
  and Adults with Learning
  Disabilities
P.O. Box 3303
2740 South Glenstone
Springfield, MO 65808
(417) 864-5110

Montana

Montana Association for Children
  and Adults with Learning
  Disabilities
3024 Macona Lane
Billings, MT 59102
(406) 252-4845

Nebraska

Nebraska Association for Children
and Adults with Learning
Disabilities
P.O. Box 6464
Omaha, NE 68106
(402) 571-7771

New Hampshire

New Hampshire Association for
Children and Adults with
Learning Disabilities
20 Wedgewood Drive
Concord, NH 03307

New Jersey

New Jersey Association for Children
and Adults with Learning
Disabilities
P.O. Box 3241
Margate, NJ 08402
(609) 822-4082

New Mexico

ADD Support Group
c/o Mountain Elementary School
2280 North Road
Los Alamos, NM 87544-1798
(505) 662-4367

New York

New York Association for the
Learning Disabled
90 S. Swan St.
Albany, NY 12210
(518) 436-4633

North Carolina

Learning Disabilities Association of
North Carolina
P.O. Box 3542

Chapel Hill, NC 27515-3542
(919) 967-9537

North Dakota

North Dakota Learning Disabilities
Association
7 East Central Avenue, #202
Minot, ND 58701
(701) 852-6665

Ohio

Ohio Association for Children and
Adults with Learning Disabilities
1480 Pearl Rd., #5
Brunswick, OH
44212

Oklahoma

Oklahoma Association for Children
and Adults with Learning
Disabilities
3701 N.W. 62d Street
Oklahoma City, OK 73112
(405) 943-9434

Oregon

Learning Disabilities Association for
Children and Adults
3903 SW Kelly
Portland, OR 97201
(503) 229-4439

Rhode Island

Rhode Island Association for
Children and Adults with
Learning Disabilities
P.O. Box 6685
Providence, RI 02904

South Dakota

South Dakota Parent Connection
P.O. Box 84813
Sioux Falls, SD 57118
(605) 335-8844

Tennessee

Tennessee Association for Children
and Adults with Learning
Disabilities
P.O. Box 111199
Memphis, TN 38111
(901) 323-1430

Knoxville Association for Children
and Adults with Learning
Disabilities
P.O. Box 23242
Knoxville, TN 37933
(615) 544-3462

Texas

Attention-Deficit Hyperactivity
Disorder Association of Texas
P.O. Box 61592
Houston, TX 77208-1592
(713) 955-3720

Vermont

Vermont Association for the Learning Disabled
9 Heaton Street
Montpelier, VT 05602
(801) 223-5480

Virginia

HAAD
106 South Street
Suite 207
Charlottesville, VA

Washington

Washington Association for
Children and Adults with
Learning Disabilities
Suite 100
17530 N.W. Union Hill Road
Redmond, WA 98052
(206) 822-0792

Wisconsin

Wisconsin Association for
Hyperactive Children
P.O. Box 1477
Milwaukee, WI 53201-1477
(414) 332-6162

Index